ON ACTORS

AND

THE ART OF ACTING

BY

GEORGE HENRY LEWES

GREENWOOD PRESS, PUBLISHERS
WESTPORT, CONNECTICUT

Originally published in 1957 by Grove Press

Reprinted with the permission of Grove Press, Inc.

Reprinted in 1968 by Greenwood Press
A division of Congressional Information Service
88 Post Road West, Westport, Connecticut 06881

Library of Congress Catalog Card Number 68-56038

ISBN 0-8371-0533-1

Printed in the United States of America

10 9 8 7 6 5 4 3 2

EPISTLE TO ANTHONY TROLLOPE.

My Dear Trollope:

One reason for inscribing this trifle to you is that
years ago you expressed a wish to see some dramatic
criticisms which had interested you republished in a
more accessible form than the pages of a periodical.
The reasons which have always deterred me from re-
publishing articles written for a temporary purpose
have not lost their force; and if I here weave together
several detached papers into a small volume, it is because a temporary purpose may again be served now a
change seems coming over the state of the stage, and
there are signs of a revival of the once splendid art of
the actor. To effect this revival there must be not
only accomplished artists and an eager public; there
must be a more enlightened public. The critical pit,
filled with play-goers who were familiar with fine acting
and had trained judgments, has disappeared. In its
place there is a mass of amusement-seekers, not without a nucleus of intelligent spectators, but of this
nucleus only a small minority has very accurate ideas
of what constitutes good art.

The performances of Salvini this summer, while
reawakening my slumbering interest in the stage, recalling the fine raptures of bygone years, have also,

by the discussions to which they have led, made me
sensible of the chaotic state of opinion on the subject
of acting in many minds of rare intelligence. I have
heard those for whose opinions in other directions my
respect is great utter judgments on this subject which
proved that they had not even a suspicion of what
the art of acting really is. Whether they blamed or
praised, the grounds which they advanced for praise
and blame were often questionable. Every reader
will admit that, without knowing anything of the art
of painting, each visitor at the exhibition is at perfect
liberty to express his admiration or dislike of any picture, so long as he confines himself to the expression
of a personal feeling, and says, "This pleases—this
displeases me." But it is preposterous (though exceedingly common) for one who has never qualified
himself by a study of the conditions and demands of
the art to formulate his personal feeling in a critical
judgment, and say, "This is a fine picture; this
painter is quite second-rate." Equally preposterous
may be the estimate of an actor on the part of those
who have not studied the art.

It is noticeable that people generally overrate a fine
actor's genius, and underrate his trained skill. They
are apt to credit him with a power of intellectual conception and poetic creation to which he has really a
very slight claim, and fail to recognize all the difficulties which his artistic training has enabled him to
master. The ordinary spectator is moved, but is incapable of discriminating the sources of his emotion: he
identifies the actor with the character, and assigns to
the actor's genius the effect mainly due to the dram-

atist. Nor is this illusion dispelled when, on some other occasion, this same actor leaves him quite unmoved by a representation of similar passions not rendered æsthetically truthful by the dramatist. Thousands have been moved by performers in Hamlet, whose acting in other characters has excited indifference or contempt. The fact that no actor has been known utterly to fail in Hamlet, while failures in Shylock and Othello are numerous, is very instructive. I remember when the German company played "Faust" at the St. James's Theatre, the sudden illness of the tragedian who was to have played Mephistopheles caused the part to be handed over to a fourth-rate member of the troupe who knew the part; yet although the performance was a very poor example of the art, the interest excited by the character was so great that the public and the critics were delighted. It is the incalculable advantage of the actor that he stands in the suffused light of emotion kindled by the author. He speaks the great thoughts of an impassioned mind, and is rewarded, as the bearer of glad tidings is rewarded, though he have had nothing to do with the facts which he narrates.

Another general misconception is that there is no special physique nor any special training necessary to make an actor. Almost every young person imagines he could act, if he tried. There is a story of some one who, on being asked if he could play the violin, answered, "I don't know; I never tried." This is the ordinary view of acting. The answer should have been, "No, I cánnot play, *because* I never tried." Violin-playing and acting do not come by nature.

Nor is t any argument that private theatricals (a very pleasant amusement—for the performers) often reveal a certain amount of histrionic aptitude in people who have never been trained. In the first place, the amateur is always a copy of some actors he has seen. In the next place, amateur acting bears the same relation to the art of the stage as drawing-room singing bears to the opera. We often listen with pleasure to a singer in private whom we should mercilessly hiss from the concert-room or stage.

The non-recognition of the difficulties of the art arises from a non-recognition of the conditions under which the artist produces his effects. We must know what are the demands and limitations of scenic presentation before we can decide whether the actor has shown skill. Ignorance of these sustains the current confusions respecting *natural* acting. Ignorance of these assigns excellences or deficiencies to the actor's mind, when in reality they depend solely on his means of physical expression. If there is no pathos in the tones, the actor's soul may be a sob, yet we shall remain unmoved. The poet, who felt that pathos when he wrote, would probably be ridiculous were he in the actor's place, and tried to give expression to the feeling.

But I must not be seduced into a dissertation. I only wanted to indicate that the object of here reprinting remarks, made at various times and in various periodicals, is to call upon the reflective part of the public to make some attempt at discriminating the sources of theatrical emotion. I want to direct attention not simply to the fact that acting is an art, but that, like all other arts, it is obstructed by a mass of unsystematized opinion, calling itself criticism.

You will understand how there must necessarily be repetitions, in articles written on the same subject at widely different periods; and how the treatment of each subject can never pretend to be exhaustive in periodical papers. Let me, in conclusion, add that they were written during a period of dramatic degradation. The poetic drama had vanished with Macready and Helen Faucit, and its day seemed, to many, a day which would never recur. With "Hamlet" and "Othello" drawing enthusiastic crowds during a long season, and with a play by Tennyson promised for the next, the day, let us hope, has once more dawned!

Ever yours affectionately,

G. H. LEWES.

CONTENTS.

ON ACTORS

AND

THE ART OF ACTING.

———

CHAPTER I.

EDMUND KEAN.

THE greatest artist is he who is greatest in the highest reaches of his art, even although he may lack the qualities necessary for the adequate execution of some minor details. It is not by his faults, but by his excellences, that we measure a great man. The strength of a beam is measured by its weakest part, of a man by his strongest. Thus estimated, Edmund Kean was incomparably the greatest actor I have seen, although even warm admirers must admit that he had many and serious defects. His was not a flexible genius. He was a very imperfect mime—or more correctly speaking, his miming power, though admirable within a certain range, was singularly limited in its range. He was tricky and flashy in style. But he was an actor of such splendid endowments in the highest departments of the art, that no one in our day can be named

of equal rank, unless it be Rachel, who was as a woman what he was as a man. The irregular splendor of
his power was felicitously characterized in the saying
of Coleridge, that "seeing Kean act was reading Shakspeare by flashes of lightning," so brilliant and so
startling were the sudden illuminations, and so murky
the dull intervals. Critics who had formed their ideal
on the Kemble school were shocked at Kean's want
of dignity, and at his fitful elocution, sometimes
thrillingly effective, at other times deplorably tame
and careless; in their angry protests they went so far
as to declare him "a mere mountebank." Not so
thought the pit; not so thought less biased critics.
He stirred the general heart with such a rush of
mighty power, impressed himself so vividly by accent,
look and gesture, that it was as vain to protest against
his defects as it was for French critics to insist upon
Shakspeare's want of *bienséance* and *bon goût*. Could
audiences have remained unmoved, they might have
lent a willing ear to remonstrances, and laughed at or
hissed some grave offences against taste and sense.
But no audience could be unmoved; all defects were
overlooked or disregarded, because it was impossible
to watch Kean as Othello, Shylock, Richard, or Sir
Giles Overreach, without being strangely shaken by
the terror, and the pathos, and the passion of a stormy
spirit uttering itself in tones of irresistible power. His
imitators have been mostly ridiculous, simply because
they reproduced the manner and the mannerism, but
could not reproduce the power which made these en-
durable. It is a fact little understood by imitators
that the spots on the sun in nowise warm the world,

and that a deficiency in light and heat cannot be replaced by a prodigality of spots.

Although I was a little boy when I first saw Kean, in 1825, and but a youth when, in 1832, he quitted the stage for ever, yet so ineffaceable are the impressions his acting produced, that I feel far more at ease in speaking of his excellences and defects than I should feel in speaking of many actors seen only a dozen years ago. It will be understood that I was in no condition then to form an estimate of his qualities, and that I criticise from memory. Yet my memory of him is so vivid that I see his looks and gestures and hear his thrilling voice as if these were sensations of yesterday. Perhaps the defects which I now recognize would be more salient were I now to witness the performances. There is a softening, idealizing tendency in memory which may exaggerate the degree of excellence. Still these are only matters of degree; and I think that my appreciation of the actor is on the whole little disturbed by such influences. At any rate, I will try to set down fairly what a retrospect discloses.

Kean's range of expression, as already hinted, was very limited. His physical aptitudes were such as confined him to the strictly tragic passions; and for these he was magnificently endowed. Small and insignificant in figure, he could at times become impressively commanding by the lion-like power and grace of his bearing. I remember, the last time I saw him play Othello, how puny he appeared beside Macready, until in the third act, when roused by Iago's taunts and insinuations, he moved towards him with a gouty hobble, seized him by the throat, and, in a well-known explosion,

"Villain! be sure you prove," etc., seemed to swell into a stature which made Macready appear small. On that very evening, when gout made it difficult for him to display his accustomed grace, when a drunken hoarseness had ruined the once matchless voice, such was the irresistible pathos—manly, not tearful—which vibrated in his tones and expressed itself in look and gestures, that old men leaned their heads upon their arms and fairly sobbed. It was, one must confess, a patchy performance considered as a whole; some parts were miserably tricky, others misconceived, others gabbled over in haste to reach the "points"; but it was irradiated with such flashes that I would again risk broken ribs for the chance of a good place in the pit to see anything like it.

Even in earlier and better days there was much in his performance of Othello which was spasmodic, slovenly, false. The address to the Senate was very bad. He had little power of elocution unless when sustained by a strong emotion; and this long simple narrative was the kind of speech he could not manage at all. He gabbled over it, impatient to arrive at the phrase, "And this is all the witchcraft I have used. Here comes the lady, let her witness it." His delivery of this "point" always startled the audience into applause by its incisive tone and its abrupt transition; yet nothing could be more out of keeping with the Shakspearian character. Othello might smile with lofty disdain at the accusation of witchcraft, or rebut it calmly, but not make it the climax of a withering sarcasm—attacking the word "witchcraft" with high and sudden emphasis, and dropping into an almost disrespectful colloquialism as the lady appeared. Indeed, throughout the first and second acts, with the exception of occasional flashes (as in the passionate fervor with which he greets Desdemona on landing at Cyprus), Kean's Othello was rather irritating and disappointing—arresting the mind, but not satisfying it. From the third act onwards all was wrought out with a mastery over the resources of expression such as has been seldom approached. In the successive unfolding of these great scenes he represented with incomparable effect the lion-like fury, the deep and haggard pathos, the forlorn sense of desolation, alternating with gusts of stormy cries for vengeance, the misgivings and sudden reassurances, the calm and deadly resolution of one not easily moved, but who, being moved, was stirred to the very depths.

Kean was a consummate master of passionate expression. People generally spoke of him as a type of the "impulsive actor." But if by this they meant one who abandoned himself to the impulse of the moment, without forethought of pre-arranged effect, nothing could be wider from the mark. He was an artist, and in art all effects are regulated. The original suggestion may be, and generally is, sudden and unprepared—"inspired," as we say; but the alert intellect recognizes its truth, seizes on it, regulates it. Without nice calculation no proportion could be preserved; we should have a work of fitful impulse, not a work of enduring art. Kean vigilantly and patiently rehearsed every detail, trying the tones until his ear was satisfied, practicing looks and gestures until his artistic sense was satisfied; and having once regulated these he never changed them. The consequence was that, when he was sufficiently sober to stand and speak, he could act his part with the precision of a singer who has thoroughly learned his air. One who often acted with him informed me that when Kean was rehearsing on a new stage he accurately counted the number of steps he had to take before reaching a certain spot, or before uttering a certain word; these steps were justly regarded by him as part of the mechanism which could no more be neglected than the accompaniment to an air could be neglected by a singer. Hence it was that he was always the same; not always in the same health, not always in the same vigor, but always master of the part, and expressing it through the same symbols. The voice on some nights would be more irresistibly touching in "But, oh! the pity of it, Iago!"—or more musically forlorn in "Othello's occupation gone"—or more terrible in "Blood, Iago; blood, blood!" but always the accent and rhythm were unchanged; as a Tamberlik may deliver the C from the chest with more sonority one night than another, but always delivers it from the chest, and never from the head.

Kean was not only remarkable for the intensity of passionate expression, but for a peculiarity I have never seen so thoroughly realized by another, although it is one which belongs to the truth of passion, namely, the expression of *subsiding emotion.* Although fond, far too fond, of abrupt transitions— passing from vehemence to familiarity, and mingling strong lights and shadows with Caravaggio force of unreality—nevertheless his instinct taught him what few actors are taught—that a strong emotion, after discharging itself in one massive current, continues for a time expressing itself in feebler currents. The waves are not stilled when the storm has passed away. There remains the ground-swell troubling the deeps. In watching Kean's quivering muscles and altered tones you felt the subsidence of passion. The voice might be calm, but there was a tremor in it; the face might be quiet, but there were vanishing traces of the recent agitation.

One of his means of effect—sometimes one of his tricks—was to make long pauses between certain phrases. For instance, on quitting the scene, Sir Edward Mortimer has to say warningly, "Wilford, remember!" Kean used to pause after "Wilford," and during the pause his face underwent a rapid succession of expressions fluently melting into each other, and all tending to one climax of threat; and then the deep tones of "remember!" came like muttered thunder. Those spectators who were unable to catch these expressions considered the pause a mere trick; and sometimes the pauses were only tricks, but often they were subtle truths.

Having been trained to the stage from his childhood, and being endowed with a remarkably graceful person, he was a master of scenic effect. He largely increased the stock of "business," which is the tradition of the stage. Hamlet, Othello, Richard, Shylock, Lear, Sir Giles Overreach, or Sir Edward Mortimer have been illuminated by him in a way neither actors

nor play-goers commonly suspect. It is his reading
of the parts, his "points," that we applaud. He was
a real innovator. But the parts he could play were
few. He had no gaiety; he could not laugh; he had
no playfulness that was not as the playfulness of
a panther showing her claws every moment. Of this
kind was the gaiety of his Richard III. Who can
ever forget the exquisite grace with which he leaned
against the side-scene while Anne was railing at him,
and the chuckling mirth of his " Poor fool! what pains
she takes to damn herself!" It was thoroughly
feline—terrible yet beautiful.

He had tenderness, wrath, agony, and sarcasm at
command. But he could not be calmly dignified; nor
could he represent the intellectual side of heroism.
He was nothing if not passionate. I never saw his
Hamlet, which, however, was never considered one of
his successes, though parts were intensely admired.
He must have been puzzled what to do with many of the
long speeches and the quiet scenes, and could have had
no sympathy with the character. Yet Hamlet is the
easiest of all Shakspeare's great parts for an actor of
moderate ability. Othello, which is the most trying
of all Shakspeare's parts, was Kean's masterpiece.
His Shylock was freer from fault, and indeed was a
marvellous performance. From the first moment
that he appeared and leant upon his stick to listen
gravely while moneys are requested of him, he impressed the audience, as Douglas Jerrold used to say,
"like a chapter of Genesis." The overpowering re-
monstrant sarcasm of his address to Antonio, and the
sardonic mirth of his proposition about the "merry

bond," were fine preparations for the anguish and
rage at the elopement of his daughter, and for the
gloating anticipations of revenge on the Christians.
Anything more impressive than the passionate re-
crimination and wild justice of argument in his
" Hath not a Jew eyes?" has never been seen on our
stage.

CHAPTER II.

CHARLES KEAN.

TO speak of the son immediately after the father is not only to follow out a natural suggestion, but to seize an excellent opportunity of elucidating some characteristics of both. It may press a little hard upon Charles Kean, but from the first he has been subject to this overshadowing comparison. Like his father, he is an accomplished swordsman, and thorough master of all the business of the stage; like his father, he is endowed with great physical force, and is capable of abandoning himself to the wildest expression of it without peril of a breakdown. Unlike his father, he is never careless; he anxiously elaborates every scene to the utmost in his power, never throwing a chance away, never failing except from lack of means. He is not only a respectable and respected member of his profession; he has the real artist's love of his art, and pride in it, and he always does his best. Laughed at, ridiculed, and hissed, and for many years terribly handled by critics, both in public and private, he has worked steadily, resolutely, improvingly, till his brave perseverance has finally conquered an eminent position. He began by being a very bad actor; he has ended by forcing even such of his critics as have least sympathy with him to admit that in certain parts he is without a rival on our stage. This battle with the public he has fought by inches. Slowly the force that is in him, concentrated on the one object of his life, has made an actor out of very unpromising materials. His career is a lesson. It shows what can and what cannot be done by courageous devotion and a burning desire to learn the resources of an art. The stamping, spluttering, ranting, tricky actor, who in his "sallet days" excited so much mirth and so much blame, has become remarkable for the naturalness and forcible quietness with which he plays certain parts. He is still unhappily given to rant when he has to express strong emotion; but rant is the resource of incompetence in all actors of tragic characters; and it is only on occasions of excitement that he falls into this mistake. On other occasions he is calm and forcible.

I must confess that it has never been an intellectual treat to me to see Charles Kean play Shakspeare's tragic heroes, but I doubt whether even his great father could have surpassed him in certain melodramatic parts. I am unable to speak of his Louis XI.— by many considered his finest performance—but I can easily believe that it was as superior to the representation of Ligier, on which it was modeled, as his performance of the Corsican Brothers was to that of Fechter, which also served him as a model. In the lighter scenes of the two first acts of the "Corsican Brothers" he wanted the graceful ease of Fechter; but in the more serious scenes, and throughout the third act, he surpassed the Frenchman with all the weight and intensity of a tragic actor in situations for which the comedian is unsuited. The deadly quiet of a strong nature, nerved to a great catastrophe— the sombre, fatal, pitiless expression—could not have been more forcibly given than by Charles Kean in this act; and in the duel there was a stealthy intensity in every look and movement, which gave a shuddering fascination to the scenes altogether missed by Fechter. In " Pauline," also, Charles Kean showed similar power—quiet and terrible. Both his qualities and defects conspired to make these performances singularly effective, and revealed a first-rate melodramatic actor where hitherto we had known only a bad tragedian.

To some of my readers it may not be at first evident how an actor can be really great in melodrama and weak in tragedy. Yet they will have no difficulty in understanding that a man may write admirable melodramas without even moderate success in attempting tragedies. The very qualities which ensure excellence in the one prepare the failure in the other. The tragic poet includes the melodramatist. Strip " Hamlet " and " Macbeth " of their poetry and psychology, and you have a fine melodramatic residuum. Sophocles and Shakspeare are as " sensational" as Fitzball and Dumas; but the situations, which in the latter are the aim and object of the piece, to which all the rest is subordinated, in the former are the mere starting points, the nodes of dramatic action. A melodramatic actor is required to be impressive, to paint in broad, coarse outlines, to give relief to an exaggerated situation; he is not required to be poetic, subtle, true to human emotion; for the scene he presents and the language he speaks are removed into an unreal, unideal sphere, *i. e.*, a sphere which is not that of reality nor of poetic idealism.

No sooner does Charles Kean attempt one of Shakspeare's flexible and human characters than the inflexible nature of his talent places him in conspicuous inferiority not only to his great father but to all fine actors. The fluency of Shakspeare's movements, the subtle interpenetration of thought and emotion, the tangled web of motives, the mingling of the heroic with the familiar, the presence of constant verisimilitude under exceptional and exaggerated conditions, all demand great flexibility of conception and expression in the actor, great sympathy of imagination, nicety of observation, and variety of mimetic power. In these Charles Kean is wholly deficient. He has the power of coarse painting, of impressive representation when the image to be presented is a simple one; but he has no subtlety, no nicety of observation, no variety of expression. He is peculiarly rigid—this is his force and his weakness: "he moveth altogether if he move at all." His face is utterly without physiognomical play; one stolid expression, immovable as an ancient mask, is worn throughout a scene which demands fluctuating variety. He has none of those unforgettable looks which made his father terrible to fellow-actors no less than to spectators. There has never been the smallest danger of his frightening an actress into fits, as Edmund Kean is said to have frightened Mrs. Glover—a story I suspect to be somewhat mythical, but a story which indicates the mighty power of Kean's glare and the ghastly convulsion of his rage.

It is because there is no presence of poetry in his acting that we all feel Charles Kean to be essentialiy a melodramatic actor. The unreality and unidealitv of a melodrama are alike suited to his means. If he attempt to portray real emotion, he leaves us cold; it he attempt to indicate a subtle truth, it is done so clumsily and so completely from the outside conventional view that we are distressed. He has no sympathy with what is heroic. He wants nicety of observation and expression for what is real.

Let us consider his voice, that being the actor's most potent instrument of expression. It is harsh and rasping; so, indeed, was the voice of his father in its upper range (though less so), but in its lower range it was marvellously musical, and had tones of a searching pathos never heard since. Partly because of the voice which is inflexible, but mainly because of an insensibility to rhythmic modulation, Charles Kean cannot deliver a passage with musical effect. The stubborn harshness of the voice and the mechanicalness of his elocution spoil even his best efforts. The tones of his father vibrate still in the memories of those who years ago trembled deliciously beneath their influence; and render even pathetic phrases powerless when spoken by his successors, because the successors cannot utter them with such "ravishing division." When Charles Kean as Richard delivers the speech—

Now is the winter of our discontent—

no one notices it; but who can ever forget his father's look and voice? Who can forget the thrilling effect of the rich deep note upon "buried," when with the graceful curl of the wrist he indicated how the clouds which lowered round his head were in the deep bosom of the ocean buried?

Voice, look, and gesture are the actor's symbols, through which he makes intelligible the emotions of the character he is personating. No amount of sensibility will avail unless it can express itself adequately by these symbols. It is not enough for an actor to *feel*, he must *represent*. He must express his feelings in symbols universally intelligible and affecting. A harsh, inflexible voice, a rigid or heavy face, would prevent even a Shakspeare from being impressive and affecting on the stage; whereas a man, with little sensibility, but endowed with a sympathetic, penetrating voice, and a flexible physiognomy, would rouse the pit to transports.

It is clear that Charles Kean has an organization which excludes him from the artistic *expression* of complex or subtle emotions. And it was to this I alluded in saying that his perseverance had made an actor out of very unpromising materials. There are no tears in his pathos; there is no terror in his wrath. He is violent where he should be agitating, lachrymose where he should be affecting. He has been acting tragic parts for more than thirty years; I should be very much surprised to learn that he had once drawn a tear; the pathos of a situation may have sometimes overcome a susceptible spectator, but this effect is not to be set down to the actor.

The tears lie very near the surface with me, but I never felt their sources stirred by any look or tone from him.

In Edmund Kean the ground-swell of subsiding emotion was, as I have noted, very finely indicated. In Charles Kean there is no trace of it. He passes from excessive vehemence to perfect calmness, without either voice or look betraying any fluent continuity between the two. The fact is that he never imaginatively identifies himself with a passion; otherwise, even *his* stubborn physique would express something of it, though inadequately.

Edmund Kean's elocution was often careless and ineffective, especially in level passages. But his musical ear and musical voice saved him from the monotony so disagreeable in the elocution of his son, and saved him from that still more unpardonable defect, the dissociation of rhythm from meaning. Instead of making the rhythm fluent with the meaning, and allowing emphasis and pause to fall in the places where naturally the thought becomes emphatic and pauses, he suffers them to be very much determined by the *formal* structure of the verse—as if the sense ended with the line—or by the duration of his breath.

Emphasis and pause are indeed the supreme difficulties of elocution. They are rarely managed by those who read blank verse, even in a room, and on the stage the difficulty is greatly enhanced. Nevertheless no one can pretend to be an actor of the poetic drama who has not mastered this art; although at the present day it is, like many other requisites, boldly disregarded, and we hear the noblest verse spouted (not spoken) with the remorseless indifference of that actor who announced himself thus:

'Tis I, my lord, the early village cock.

Edmund Kean had no gaiety, no humor. His son, although also destitute of both, is nevertheless very comic in one or two characters, notably Ford in the "Merry Wives of Windsor." The very inflexibility of his face here gives him real comic force. Precisely because his features will not express any fluctuations of feeling, they are admirably suited to express the puzzled, wondering stolidity of the jealous, bamboozled husband. It is this inflexibility, combined with a certain animal force, which makes his melodramat.c personations so effective.

Edmund Kean did much for Shakspeare. The acting edition of our great dramatist may now almost be said to be based upon his conceptions of the leading parts. He invented much. His own quick, passionate sympathy saw effects where other actors had seen nothing. But I suspect that he had only the actor's feeling for the dramatist, and cared little about him as a poet. Charles Kean has more literary culture, and has shown a more literary ambition. He has added nothing to the elucidation of the characters, he has given no fresh light to players or public; but he has greatly improved the scenic representation, and has lavished time and money on the archæological illustration of the plays. He has striven for public applause by appealing to the public taste, and he has gained that applause. Those who, like myself, care a great deal about acting and very little about splendid dresses, must nevertheless confess that what Charles Kean professed to do in the way of scenic illustration, he did splendidly and successfully.

CHAPTER III.

RACHEL.

RACHEL was the panther of the stage; with a panther's terrible beauty and undulating grace she moved and stood, glared and sprang. There always seemed something not human about her. She seemed made of different clay from her fellows—beautiful but not lovable. Those who never saw Edmund Kean may form a very good conception of him if they have seen Rachel. She was very much as a woman what he was as a man. If he was a lion, she was a panther.

Her range, like Kean's, was very limited, but her expression was perfect within that range. Scorn, triumph, rage, lust and merciless malignity she could represent in symbols of irresistible power; but she had little tenderness, no womanly caressing softness, no gaiety, no heartiness. She was so graceful and so powerful that her air of dignity was incomparable; but somehow you always felt in her presence an indefinable suggestion of latent wickedness. By the side of Pasta she would have appeared like a beautiful devil beside a queenly woman: with more intellect, more incisive and impressive power, but with less soul, less diffusive and subduing influence.

In her early days nothing more exquisite could be heard than her elocution—it was musical and artistically graduated to the fluctuations of meaning. Her thrilling voice, flexible, penetrating, and grave, responded with the precision of a keyed instrument. Her thin, nervous frame vibrated with emotion. Her face, which would have been common, had it not been aflame with genius, was capable of intense expression. Her gestures were so fluent and graceful that merely to see her would have been a rare delight. The ideal tragedies of Racine, which ignorant Englishmen call "cold," were, by her interpretation, shown to be instinct with passion and dramatic effect. But this was only in her early days. Later in her career she grew careless; played her parts as if only in a hurry to get through them, flashing out now and then with tremendous power, just to show what she could do; and resembling Kean in the sacrifice of the character to a few points. She, whose elocution had been incomparable, so delicately shaded were its various refinements and so sustained its music, came at last to gabble, and to mash up her rhythm till the verses were often unintelligible and generally ineffective. After the gabble she paused upon some well-known point, and flung upon it all the emphasis of her power. In what I have to say of her, I shall speak only of her acting in its better days, for it is that to which memory naturally recurs.

The finest of her performances was of Phédre. Nothing I have ever seen surpassed this picture of a soul torn by the conflicts of incestuous passion and struggling conscience; the unutterable mournfulness

of her look and tone as she recognized the guilt of
her desires, yet felt herself so possessed by them
that escape was impossible, are things never to be forgotten. What a picture she was as she entered!
You felt that she was wasting away under the fire
within, that she was standing on the verge of the
grave with pallid face, hot eyes, emaciated frame—an
awful ghastly apparition. The slow, deep, mournful
toning of her apostrophe to the sun, especially that
close—

> Soleil! je te viens voir pour la dernière fois—

produced a thrill which vibrates still in memory. The
whole of the opening scene, with one exception, was
inexpressibly affecting and intensely true. As an
ideal representation of real emotion, it belonged to
the highest art. The remorseful lines—

> Grâces au ciel, mes mains ne sont point criminelles:
> Plût aux dieux que mon cœur fût innocent comme elles—

were charged with pathos. And how finely expressed
was the hurrying horror with, as it were, a shiver between each phrase, transient yet vividly indicated,
when she confessed her guilt—

> Tu vas ouïr le comble des horreurs . . .
> J'aime . . . à ce nom fatal, je tremble, je frissonne . . .

(and her whole frame here quivered)

> J'aime . . .
> *Œnone.*—Qui?
> *Phédre.*—Tu connais ce fils de l'Amazone,
> Ce prince si longtemps par moi-même opprimé . . .

Œnone.—Hippolyte !   Grands dieux !
Phédre.—*C'est toi qui l'as nommé.*

The one point in this scene to which I took exception was the mode of rendering the poet's meaning in
this magnificent apostrophe, taken from Euripides,
" C'est toi qui l'as nommé."   She uttered it in a tone
of sorrowing reproach, which, as I conceive, is psychologically at variance with the character and the position.   For Phédre has kept her love a secret; it is a
horrible crime ; she cannot utter the name of Hippolyte because of her horror at the crime ; and not in
sadness, but in the sophistry of passion, she tries indignantly to throw on Œnone the guilt of naming
that which should be unnamable.

In the second act, where Phédre declares her passion to Hippolyte, Rachel was transcendent.   She
subtly contrived to indicate that her passion was a
diseased passion, fiery and irresistible, yet odious to
her and to him.   She was marvellous in the abandon-
ment to this onward-sweeping madness ; her manner
was fierce and rapid, as if the thoughts were crowding
on her brain in tumult, and she dared not pause to
consider them ; and such was the amazing variety and
compass of her expression that when she quitted the
stage she left us quivering with an excitement comparable only to that produced by Kean in the third
act of " Othello."   In the fourth act came the storm
of rage, jealousy, and despair ; it was lit up by wonderful flashes.   Like Kean, she had a power of concentrating into a single phrase a world of intense

feeling; and even Kean himself could not have surpassed the terrific exclamation—

Misérable ! et je vis !

Whoever saw Rachel play Phédre may be pardoned
if he doubt whether he will ever see such acting again.

Hermione, in " Andromaque," was also another
very fine part of hers, especially in the two great
scenes with Pyrrhus. In the first her withering sarcasm, calm, polished, implacable, was beyond description; in the second she displayed her manifold
resources in expressing rage, scorn, grief and defiance.
In her eyes charged with lightning, in her thin con-
vulsive frame, in the spasms of her voice, changing
from melodious clearness to a hoarseness that made
us shudder, the demoniac element was felt. With
touching and forlorn grace she revealed the secret of
her heart in the lines—

> Malgré le juste horreur que son crime me donne,
> Tant qu'il vivra craignez que je ne lui pardonne ;
> Doutez jusqu'à sa mort d'un courroux incertain :
> S'il ne meurt aujourd'hui *je puis l'aimer demain.*

In describing how she will avenge the insult to her
beauty by slaying Pyrrhus—

Je percerai le cœur que je n'ai pu toucher—

her wail was so piercing and so musical that the whole
audience rose in a transport to applaud her; and difficult as it was to prevent an anticlimax after such an
effect, she crowned the scene with the exclamation

of jealous threat when bidding him hasten to his mistress:

Va, cours ; mais crains encore d'y trouver Hermione

The close was in the same high strain. The fine passionate speech in which she upbraids Orestes for having followed her orders and slain Pyrrhus (a speech which may be commended to those who fancy Racine is cold) was delivered as nobody but Rachel could deliver it.

Very noticeable it is that Rachel could not speak prose with even tolerable success; deprived of the music of verse, and missing its *ictus,* she seemed quite incapable of managing the easy cadences of colloquial prose. The subtle influence of rhythm seemed to penetrate her, and gave a movement and animation to her delivery which was altogether wanting in her declamation of prose. Hence, among other reasons, the failure of her attempts in modern drama. As Kean was only truly great in Shakspeare and Massinger, Rachel was only truly herself in Racine and Corneille.

In the "Polyeucte" of Corneille she had one scene of incomparable grandeur, where, baptized in the blood of her martyred husband, she exclaims:

Son sang dont tes bourreaux viennent de me couvrir
M'a desillé les yeux, et me les vient d'ouvrir.
Je vois, je sais, je crois !

The climbing exultation and radiant glory of the inspired convert, her face lighted with fervor, her whole frame trembling with the burden of overpowering thoughts, were fitly succeeded by the uplifting of her arms to heaven, while an expression of such fervent aspiration glowed in her features that she seemed a martyr welcoming the death which was the portal to eternal bliss. As an example of "face-acting" should be cited the very remarkable scene in "Les Horaces," in which she stands silent during the long recital of her lover's death.

Rachel tried once or twice to play Molière. I did not see these attempts, which were pitilessly criti-cised by Jules Janin, but I am convinced that they were mistakes. She was wholly unsuited to comedy, un-less it were comedy like that of Madame Girardin's Lady Tartufe, in which I thought her graceful, lady-like, and diabolical—very admirable in the way she thoroughly identified herself with the character, making its odiousness appear so thoroughly easy and unconscious that you almost doubted whether after all the woman were so odious. The manner in which Rachel walked to the fireplace, placed her gloves on the mantelpiece, and her right foot on the fender, as she began the great scene with her lover, was of itself a study. The sleek hypocrisy of the part was not exaggerated, nor was the cruel irony colder or crueler than seemed natural to such a woman ; it was like the occasional gleam of it in " Bajazet," especially where Roxane is assured that Bajazet loves her still, and she replies, smiling with calm, bitter superiority—

Il y va de sa vie, au moins, que je le croie.

It would form an interesting question why actors so transcendent as Kean and Rachel should have been singularly limited in the range of characters they could play with effect—why, being confessedly great in a few difficult parts, they could not be even tolerable in many parts less difficult and demanding the same kind of talent. But as this is a question I am not prepared to answer, I content myself with calling attention to it.

CHAPTER IV.

MACREADY.

IN Edmund Kean and Rachel we recognize types of genius; in Macready I see only a man of talent, but of talent so marked and individual that it approaches very near to genius; and, indeed, in justification of those admirers who would claim for him the higher title, I may say that Tieck, whose opinion on such a matter will be received with great respect, told me that Macready seemed to him a better actor than either Kean or John Kemble; and he only saw Macready in the early part of his long and arduous career.

Of John Kemble I cannot, of course, speak. And with respect to Kean, while claiming for him the indisputable superiority in the highest reaches of his art, I should admit that he was inferior to Macready in that general flexibility of talent and in that range of intellectual sympathy which are necessary to the personation of many and various parts. In this sense Macready was the better actor. And he showed it also in another striking difference. Kean created scarcely any new parts: with the exception of Bertram, Brutus and Sir Edward Mortimer all his attempts with modern plays were more or less failures. He gave the stamp of his own great power to Shylock, Othello, Sir Giles Overreach, and Richard; but he could not infuse life into Virginius or Tell, nor would he, perhaps, have succeeded with Werner, Richelieu, Claude Melnotte, Ruy Gomez, and the fifty other parts which Macready created. It is worthy of note that Kean was greatest in the greatest parts, and seemed to require the wide range of Shakspearian passion for his arena; whereas Macready was greatest in parts like Werner, Richelieu, Iago, or Virginius, and always fell short when representing the great Shakspearian hero.

Macready had a voice powerful, extensive in compass, capable of delicate modulation in quiet passages (though with a tendency to scream in violent passages), and having tones that thrilled and tones that stirred tears. His declamation was mannered and unmusical; yet his intelligence always made him follow the winding meanings through the involutions of the verse, and never allowed you to feel, as you feel in the declamation of Charles Kean and many other actors, that he was speaking words which he did not thoroughly understand. The trick of a broken and spasmodic rhythm might destroy the music proper to the verse, but it did not perplex you with false emphasis or intonations wandering at hazard. His person was good, and his face expressive.

We shall perhaps best understand the nature of his talent by thinking of the characters he most successfully personated. They were many and various, implying great flexibility in his powers; but they were not characters of grandeur, physical or moral.

They were domestic rather than ideal, and made but slight appeals to the larger passions which give strength to heroes. He was irritable where he should have been passionate, querulous were he should have been terrible.

In Macbeth, for example, nothing could be finer than the indications he gave of a conscience wavering under the influence of "fate and metaphysical aid," superstitious, and weakly cherishing the suggestions of superstition; but nothing could have been less heroic than his presentation of the great criminal. He was fretful and impatient under the taunts and provocations of his wife; he was ignoble under the terrors of remorse; he stole into the sleeping-chamber of Duncan like a man going to purloin a purse, not like a warrior going to snatch a crown.

In Othello, again, his passion was irritability, and his agony had no grandeur. His Hamlet I thought bad, due allowance being made for the intelligence it displayed. He was lachrymose and fretful: too fond of a cambric pocket-handkerchief to be really affecting; nor, as it seemed to me, had he that sympathy with the character which would have given an impressive unity to his performance—it was "a thing of shreds and patches," not a whole. In King John, Richard II., Iago, and Cassius all his great qualities were displayed. In Werner he represented the anguish of a weak mind prostrate, with a pathos almost as remarkable as the heroic ageny of Kean's Othello. The forlorn look and wailing accent when his son retorts upon him his own plea, "Who taught me there were crimes made venial by the occasion?" are

not to be forgotten.   Nor was the fiery impatience of
his Cassius less remarkable; it was just the kind of
passion he could best express.

In tenderness Macready had few rivals.   He could
exhibit the noble tenderness of a father in Virginius,
as well as the chivalrous tenderness of a lover.   None
of the young men whom I have seen play Claude
Melnotte had the youthfulness of Macready in that
part; you lost all sense of his sixty years in the fervor and resilient buoyancy of his manner; and when
he paced up and down before the footlights, describing to the charming Pauline with whom his Melnotte
is memorably associated—Helen Faucit—the home
where love should be, his voice, look, and bearing had
an indescribable effect.   It was really a rare sight to
witness Claude Melnotte and Lear played by the
same actor in the same week.   The fretful irritability
of the senile king was admirably rendered; he *almost*
succeeded in making the character credible; and although the terrific curse was probably delivered by
Kean with incomparably more grandeur, the screaming vehemence of Macready was quite in keeping with
the irritability of the earlier scenes.

He was a thorough artist, very conscientious, very
much in earnest, and very careful about all the resources of his art.   Hence he was always picturesque
in his costume.   Often, indeed, his "get up" was
such that, to use a common phrase, he seemed to
have stepped from the canvas of one of the old
masters.

Compared with anyone we have seen since upon
our stage, Macready stands at such an immeasurable

height that there must needs be a strange perplexity
in the minds of his admirers on learning that while
Kean and Young were still upon the stage, Macready
was very frequently called "a mere melodramatic
actor." In any sense which I can affix to this phrase
it is absurd. He was by nature unsuited for some
great tragic parts; but by his intelligence he was fitted to conceive, and by his organization fitted to express *characters*, and was not like a melodramatic
actor—limited to *situations*. Surely Lear, King John,
Richard II., Cassius, and Iago are tragic parts? In
these he was great; nor could he be surpassed in certain aspects of Macbeth and Coriolanus, although he
wanted the heroic thew and sinew to represent these
characters as wholes.

He did not belong to the stately declamatory school
of Kemble, but in all parts strove to introduce as
much familiarity of detail as was consistent with ideal
presentation. His touches of "nature" were sometimes a little out of keeping with the general elevation
of the performance, and he was fond of making a
"point" by an abrupt transition from the declamatory
to the conversational; but whenever he had an emotion to depict he depicted it sympathetically and not
artificially; by which I mean that he felt himself to
be the person, and having identified himself with the
character, sought by means of the symbols of his art
to express what that character felt; he did not stand
outside the character and try to express its emotions
by the symbols which had been employed for other
characters by other actors. There is a story told of
him which may be exaggerated, or indeed may not

be true of him, but which at any rate illustrates so well the very important point now under notice that it may be repeated here. In the great scene of the third act of the "Merchant of Venice," Shylock has to come on in a state of intense rage and grief at the flight of his daughter. Now it is obviously a great trial for the actor to "strike twelve at once." He is one moment calm in the green-room, and the next he has to appear on the stage with his whole nature in an uproar. Unless he has a very mobile temperament, quick as flame, he cannot begin this scene at the proper state of white heat. Accordingly, we see actors in general come bawling and gesticulating, but leaving us unmoved because they are not moved themselves. Macready, it is said, used to spend some minutes behind the scenes, lashing himself into an imaginative rage by cursing *sotto voce*, and shaking violently a ladder fixed against the wall. To bystanders the effect must have been ludicrous. But to the audience the actor presented himself as one really agitated. He had worked himself up to the proper pitch of excitement which would enable him to express the rage of Shylock.

I have heard Madame Vestris tell a similar story of Liston, whom she overheard cursing and spluttering to himself, as he stood at the side scene waiting to go on in a scene of comic rage.

———

Let me add to this estimate of Macready's powers the brief account I wrote in 1851 of his farewell performance.

On Wednesday night this expected "solemnity," as the French phrase it, attracted an audience such as the walls of Drury have not enclosed for many a long year. Fortunately, the most rigorous precautions had been taken against overcrowding and occasion for disputes, so that the compact mass of beings was by no means chaotic. Every seat in stalls, boxes, and slips had been taken long before. Only the pit and galleries had to scramble for places, and by two o'clock the most patient and provident were waiting outside. Fancy the weariness of those four hours' attendance! Vinegar-yard and Little Russell street were dense with masses of expectant, jubilant, sibilant, "chaffing," swearing, shouting men; and there was no slight crowd to *see* the crowd.

As an immense favor, I was offered two places in the "basket" (as they call it), at the back of the uppermost boxes; and, in the innocence of my heart, I paid for those places, into which I would not have crammed a dog of any gentility. But I was rescued from this rehearsal of purgatory without its poetry, by the beneficence of a friend whose private box was almost as capacious as his generosity; so that, instead of an imperfect view of the scene, I commanded the whole house. And what a sight that was! how glorious, triumphant, affecting, to see every one starting up, waving hats and handkerchiefs, stamping, shouting, yelling their friendship at the great actor, who now made his appearance on that stage where he was never more to reappear! There was a *crescendo* of excitement enough to have overpowered the nerves of the most self-possessed; and when after an ener-

getic fight—which showed that the actor's powers
bore him gallantly up to the last—he fell pierced by
Macduff's sword, this death, typical of the actor's
death, this last look, this last act of the actor, struck
every bosom with a sharp and sudden blow, loosen-
ing a tempest of tumultuous feeling such as made
applause an ovation.

Some little time was suffered to elapse wherein we
recovered from the excitement, and were ready again
to burst forth as Macready the Man, dressed in his
plain black, came forward to bid "Farewell, a long
farewell to all his greatness." As he stood there,
calm but sad, waiting till the thunderous reverbera-
tions of applause should be hushed, there was one
little thing which brought the tears into my eyes,
viz., the crape hat-band and black studs, that seemed
to me more mournful and more touching than all this
vast display of sympathy: it made me forget the
paint and tinsel, the artifice and glare of an actor's
life, to remember how thoroughly that actor was a
man—one of us, sharer of sorrows we all have known
or all must know!

Silence was obtained at last; and then in a quiet,
sad tone, Macready delivered this address:

"My last theatrical part is played, and, in accordance with long-established usage, I appear once more
before you. Even if I were without precedent for
the discharge of this act of duty, it is one which my
own feelings would irresistibly urge upon me; for, as
I look back on my long professional career, I see in it
but one continuous record of indulgence and support
extended to me, cheering me in my onward progress,

and upholding me in most trying emergencies. I
have, therefore, been desirous of offering you my
parting acknowledgments for the partial kindness
with which my humble efforts have uniformly been
received, and for a life made happy by your favor.
The distance of five-and-thirty years has not dimmed
my recollection of the encouragement which gave
fresh impulse to the inexperienced essays of my youth,
and stimulated me to perseverance when struggling
hardly for equality of position with the genius and
talent of those artists whose superior excellence I un-
grudgingly admitted, admired, and honored. That
encouragement helped to place me, in respect to priv-
ileges and emolument, on a footing with my distinguished competitors. With the growth of time your
favor seemed to grow; and undisturbed in my hold
on your opinion, from year to year I found friends
more closely and thickly clustering round me. All
I can advance to testify how justly I have apprecia-
ted the patronage thus liberally awarded me is the
devotion throughout those years of my best energies
to your service. My ambition to establish a theatre,
in regard to decorum and taste, worthy of our
country, and to leave in it the plays of our divine
Shakspeare fitly illustrated, was frustrated by those
whose duty it was, in virtue of the trust committed
to them, themselves to have undertaken the task.
But some good seed has yet been sown; and in the
zeal and creditable productions of certain of our
present managers we have assurance that the corrupt
editions and unseemly presentations of past days will
never be restored, but that the purity of our great

poet's text will henceforward be held on our English stage in the reverence it ever should command. I have little more to say. By some the relation of an actor to his audience is considered slight and transient. I do not feel it so. The repeated manifestation, under circumstances personally affecting me, of your favorable sentiments towards me, will live with life among my most grateful memories; and, because I would not willingly abate one jot in your esteem, I retire with the belief of yet unfailing powers, rather than linger on the scene, to set in contrast the feeble style of age with the more vigorous exertions of my better years. Words—at least such as I can command—are ineffectual to convey my thanks. In offering them, you will believe I feel far more than I give utterance to. With sentiments of the deepest gratitude I take my leave, bidding you, ladies and gentlemen, in my professional capacity, with regret and most respectfully, farewell."

This was received with renewed applause. Perhaps a less deliberate speech would have better suited the occasion; a few words full of the eloquence of the moment would have made a deeper and more memorable impression; but under such trying circumstances a man may naturally be afraid to trust himself to the inspiration of the moment. Altogether I must praise Macready for the dignity with which he retired, and am glad that he did not *act*. There was no ostentation of cambric sorrow; there was no well got-up broken voice to simulate emotion. The manner was calm, grave, sad, and dignified.

Macready retires into the respect of private life.
A reflection naturally arises on the perishableness of
an actor's fame. He leaves no monument behind
him but his name. This is often thought a hardship.
I believe that great confusion exists in the public
mind on this subject.

It is thought a hardship that great actors in quitting the stage can leave no monument more solid
than a name. The painter leaves behind him pictures to attest his power; the author leaves behind
him books; the actor leaves only a tradition. The
curtain falls—the artist is annihilated. Succeeding
generations may be told of his genius; none can
test it.

All this I take to be a most misplaced sorrow.
With the best wishes in the world I cannot bring myself to place the actor on a level with the painter or
the author. I cannot concede to the actor such a
parity of intellectual greatness; while, at the same
time, I am forced to remember that, with inferior
abilities, he secures far greater reward, both of pud-
ding and praise. It is not difficult to assign the
causes of an actor's superior reward, both in noisy reputation and in solid guineas. He amuses. He amuses
more than the most amusing author. And our lux-
uries always cost us more than our necessities. Tag-
lioni or Carlotta were better paid than Edmund Kean
or Macready; Jenny Lind better than both put
together.

But while the dramatic artist appeals to a larger audience, and moves them more forcibly than either
painter or author, owing to the very nature of his art,

a very slight acquaintance with acting and actors will suffice to show there can be no parity in the rank of a great painter and a great actor. Place Kean beside Caravaggio (and, though I select the greatest actor I have known, I take a third-rate painter, not wishing to overpower the argument with such names as Raphael, Michel Angelo, Titian), and ask what comparison can be made of their intellectual qualifications! Or take Macready and weigh him in the scale with Bulwer or Dickens.

The truth is, we exaggerate the talent of an actor because we judge only from the effect he produces, without enquiring too curiously into the means. But, while the painter has nothing but his canvas and the author has nothing but white paper and printer's ink with which to produce his effects, the actor has all other arts as handmaids: the poet labors for him, creates his part, gives him his eloquence, his music, his imagery, his tenderness, his pathos, his sublimity; the scene-painter aids him; the costumes, the lights, the music, all the fascinations of the stage—all subserve the actor's effect: these raise him upon a pedestal; remove them, and what is he? He who can make a stage mob bend and sway with his eloquence, what could he do with a real mob, no poet by to prompt him? He who can charm us with the stateliest imagery of a noble mind, when robed in the sables of Hamlet, or in the toga of Coriolanus, what can he do in coat and trousers on the world's stage? Rub off the paint, and the eyes are no longer brilliant! Reduce the actor to his intrinsic value, and then weigh him with the rivals whom he surpasses in reputation and in fortune.

If my estimate of the intrinsic value of acting is lower than seems generally current, it is from no desire to disparage an art I have always loved; but from a desire to state what seems to me the simple truth on the matter, and to show that the demand for posthumous fame is misplaced. Already the actor gets more fame than he deserves, and we are called upon to weep that he gets no more. During his reign the applause which follows him exceeds in intensity that of all other claimants for public approbation; so long as he lives he is an object of strong sympathy and interest; and when he dies he leaves behind him such influence upon his art as his genius may have effected (true fame!) and a monument to kindle the emulation of successors. Is not that enough? Must *he* weep because other times will not see his acting? Must *we* weep because all that energy, labor, genius, if you will, is no more than a tradition? Folly!* In this crowded world how few there are who can leave even a name, how rare those who leave more. The author can be read by future ages! Oh! yes, he *can* be read: the books are preserved; but *is* he read? Who disturbs them from their repose upon the dusty shelves of silent libraries?

---

* The illustrious mathematician, Jacobi, in his old age, was once consoled by a flattering disciple with the remark that all future mathematicians would delight in his work. He drew down the corners of his mouth and said, despairingly, "Yes; but to think that all my predecessors knew nothing of my work!" Here was vanity hungrier than that of the actor.

What are the great men of former ages, with rare, very rare, exceptions, but *names* to the world which shelves their well-bound volumes!

Unless some one will tell me in sober gravity (what is sometimes absurdly said in fulsome dinner speeches and foolish dedications) that the actor has a " kindred genius" with the poet, whose creations he represents, and that in sheer intellectual calibre Kean and Macready were nearly on a par with Shakspeare, I do not see what cause of complaint can exist in the actor's not sharing the posthumous fame of a Shakspeare. His fame while he lives surpasses that of almost all other men. Byron was not so widely worshiped as Kean. Lawrence and Northcote, Wilkie and Mulready, what space did they fill in the public eye compared with Young, Charles Kemble, or Macready? Surely this renown is ample?

If Macready share the regret of his friends, and if he yearn for posthumous fame, there is yet one issue for him to give the world assurance of his powers. Shakspeare is a good raft whereon to float securely down the stream of time; fasten yourself to that and your immortality is safe. Now Shakspeare must have occupied more of Macready's time and thought than any other subject. Let fruits be given. Let us have from him an edition of Shakspeare, bringing all his practical experience as an actor to illustrate this the first of dramatists. We want no more black letter. We want no more hyperboles of admiration. We want the *dramatic* excellence and defects illustrated and set forth. Will Macready undertake such a task? It would be a delightful *object* to occupy his leisure; and it would settle the question as to his own intellectual claims.

The foregoing was written in 1851. This year, 1875, the "Reminiscences and Diaries of Macready" have been given to the world by Sir Frederick Pollock, and they strikingly confirm the justice of my estimate, which almost reads like an echo of what Macready himself expressed. In those volumes we see the incessant study which this eminently conscientious man to the last bestowed on every detail connected with his art; we see also how he endeavored by study to make up for natural deficiencies, and how conscious he was of these deficiencies. We see him over-sensitive to the imaginary disrespect in which his profession is held, and throughout his career hating the stage, while devoting himself to the art. But although his sensitiveness suffered from many of the external conditions of the player's life, his own acceptance by the world was a constant rebuke to his exaggerated claims. He was undeniably a cultivated, honorable, and able man, and would have made an excellent clergyman or member of Parliament; but there is absolutely no evidence that he could have made such a figure either in the Church or Senate as would compare with that which he made upon the stage.

CHAPTER V.

FARREN.

THAT no one has been found to take the place of Farren has frequently been matter of regretful reproach on the part of critics and play-goers who forget that during the memory of living men no English actor has had the slightest pretension to rank with this rare and accomplished comedian. If we of this generation have seen no other Sir Peter Teazle and Lord Ogleby, our fathers were no luckier. Farren, who began playing the old men at nineteen, and played them without a rival for nearly half a century, used to say of himself that he was a " cock salmon," the only fish of his kind in the market. And it would be a curious subject of inquiry why this was the case. In France they have had a few brilliant and many excellent representatives of what used to be called the " Farren parts." In Germany these parts have been filled as well as others ; but in England Farren has been without a rival, without even a modest rival. Blanchard, Dowton, Fawcett, Bartley, are names which linger in the memories of play-goers—all good actors in their way, but not one of them conceivable in Sir Peter Teazle or Bertrand (in " Bertrand et

Raton"), Grandfather Whitehead, or the Country
Squire (I purposely name parts embracing a wide
range); and as to the "old men" who have come
since—*non ragioniam di lor!*

There was a certain elegance and distinction about
Farren which made people constantly compare him
with the best French actors. He had a marvellous
eye for costume, and a quick appreciation of all the
little details of manner. His face was handsome,
with a wonderful hanging under-lip, capable of a great
variety of expression; he had a penetrating voice, a
clear articulation, a singularly expressive laugh; and
these qualities, coupled with a very close observation
of characteristics, made him a finished actor—whom
nobody cared about.

When I say that nobody cared about him, I mean
that, in spite of the unquestioned admiration of his
talent, there was none of that personal regard usually
felt for public favorites. Everybody applauded him;
everybody admitted his excellences; everybody was
glad to find his name on the bill, but no one went
especially to see him. In theatrical phrase "he never
drew a house." He would always "strengthen a
cast," and has many a time determined the success
of a piece. But that kind of fanaticism which popular actors excite in their admirers was never excited
by him; and I believe it was on this ground that he
so rarely visited the provinces, where other actors
reap the harvests sown in metropolitan reputations.

Why was this? Farren amused the public, and
the public applauded him. Why was he less of a
personal favorite than many an inferior actor? It

was owing, I conceive, to the parts he played, and to his manner of playing them. The parts were not those which appeal to general sympathy—they represented old age as either ridiculous or fretful, not venerable or pathetic. Crusty old bachelors, jealous old husbands, stormy fathers, worrying uncles, or ancient fops with ghastly pretensions to amiability— such were the types which he usually presented to the public; and when the types were more amiable or more humorous, there was a something in his manner which arrested a perfect sympathy. He had no geniality; he had no gaiety. There was none of the fervid animation which acts like electricity upon the spectator. He was without unction. His laugh, wonderful as a senile chuckle, or as a gurgle of sensuality, had no ring of mirth in it. The comedy was high comedy which never lowered itself to farce; but it also wanted some of the animal spirits and geniality which overflow in farce.

A striking illustration of his talent and his want of lovable humor was presented by his performance of the simple curé in "Secret Service," a translation of a French piece in which Bouffé played the same part. Those who saw the two performances hesitated as to which was the more admirable, but no one could have doubted as to which was the more lovable man, the English or the French priest. The subject of the piece is the unconscious acting as a spy by a simple-minded old curé, who, having been at school with Fouché, applies to him for some employment that he may cease to be a burden on his niece. By a mistake in interpreting Fouché's order, the curé is set to do the work of a spy, in which his innocence of manner (supposed to be art) admirably assists him. The revulsion of feeling when he discovers the truth is a good dramatic opportunity, and was pathetically rendered both by Farren and Bouffé, better by the latter because his whole organism was more sensitive. Up to this point, however, the character is one of adorable simplicity, and the way this was personated by the two great actors—each so individual, the one as English as the other was French—puzzled criticism to award the palm. But, nevertheless, we all left the theatre admiring Farren, and feeling an indefinable regard for Bouffé. I was not able to institute a similar comparison with Grandfather Whitehead, which was one of Farren's most successful performances in later years; but I suspect that a similar difference would have been noticeable.

Like all comic actors, Farren had a secret belief in his tragic powers. Nor is this general craving of comedians for acceptance in tragedy a matter for wonder or ridicule. A similar craving is felt by comic writers. It is an insurgence of self-respect against the implied disrespect of laughter. No man likes to be classed with buffoons, although he may be willing enough now and then to vent his humor in buffoonery, or to excite your admiration by his powers of mimicking what is ridiculous. There has always been to me something pathetic in the thought of Liston, with his grave and serious turn of mind, his quick sensibilities, and his intense yearning for applause, fatally classed by Nature among those to whom tragic expression was impossible—feeling

within him tragic capacity, and knowing that his face
was a grotesque mask and his voice a suggestion of
drollery. I think it not unlikely that, with another
face and voice, Liston might have succeeded in
tragedy; but this is only saying that, had he been
another man, he would have been another actor. His
mistake lay in not perceiving that, with such physical
qualifications, tragedy was impossible to him. With
Farren the case was, I imagine, still more hopeless.
The deficiency lay deeper. He could touch a chord
of pathos gently, but he was quite incapable of expressing any powerful emotion. I saw him play the
Hunchback—a part, indeed, originally intended for
him by Knowles—and never saw a fine actor so
utterly feeble. Once or twice, I believe, he tried the
experiment of Shylock upon provincial audiences;
but he was not sufficiently encouraged to try it in
London.

Farren was emphatically the representative of gentlemen. His air of high-breeding was different in
Lord Ogleby, Sir Peter Teazle, Sir Anthony Absolute, the Country Squire, and many other parts, but
it had always the seal of distinction. He was also
an actor whose fineness of observation gave an air of
intellectual superiority even to his fools. I do not
mean that he represented the fools as intellectual;
but that his manner of representing them was such
as to impress spectators with a high sense of his
intellectual finesse.

Yet I understand that in private he produced the
contrary impression. He had certainly a very keen
eye for a wide range of characteristics, and presented

a greater variety of memorable types than any actor
of his time; and if it is true, as many assert, that off
the stage he was rather stupid than otherwise, it only
shows, what indeed requires no fresh proof, that
acting is an art very much more dependent on special
aptitudes than on general intellectual vigor. A man
may be a magnificent singer with the smallest philo-
sophical endowments, and a marvellous actor with an
amount of information which would deeply afflict
Mrs. Marcet, or of critical insight which would excite
the pity of a quarterly reviewer. We are too apt to
generalize from a general term : we call a man clever
because he surpasses his rivals : and as the word clever
is used to designate any kind of superiority, we rashly
conclude that a clever actor ought to be intellectually
distinguished, and because he is a good mime he must
be an acute thinker.

Farren, undoubtedly, had in a high degree the intelligence necessary for his art, and the physical qualifications which the art demanded ; whatever he may
have been in private, he was eminently an intellectual
actor, meaning by that phrase an actor who produced
his effects not by the grotesqueness or drollery of his
physique, but by the close observation and happy reproduction of characteristics—*i. e.*, not by appealing
physically to our mirthful sensibilities, but indirectly
through our intellectual recognition of the incongruous.

CHAPTER VI.

CHARLES MATHEWS.

IT has long been the opinion of play-goers and critics that Charles Mathews might fairly be classed with the best French actors in his own line ; and the success which during two seasons he has achieved on the French stage is a striking confirmation of that opinion. Although he has been a great favorite with our public from the first night through the whole of his career, it is only of late years that he has displayed remarkable powers as a comedian. He was admired for his grace and elegance, his ease and pleasant vivacity, and for a certain versatile power of mimicry : but critics denied that he was a comedian. and I do not think the critics were unjust, so long as he confined himself to what are called "character pieces," and did not show his powers in "character parts." The difference between his performances in "He Would be an Actor" or "Patter *versus* Clatter," and in "The Game of Speculation" or "The Day of Reckoning," is all the difference between a clever mimic and a fine comedian—between a lively caricaturist and a skilful portrait-painter.

I have followed the career of this actor with de-

light. His first appearance, in "Old and Young
Stagers," forms a pleasant landing-place in my memory as I wander backwards. The incomparable
Liston delayed his departure from the stage in order
to protect the *début* of the son of his old colleague and
friend, and there have been few *débuts* more curiously
expected and more cordially welcomed. It was
known to "the boxes" that Charles Mathews had
been made a pet of in many aristocratic families, and
had acted in private circles at Rome, Florence, and
Naples with singular success. It was known to "the
pit" (in those days there were no stalls) that the son
of the public favorite, though trained as an architect,
had resolved to quit Pugin for Thespis ; and as the
Olympic, under the management of Madame Vestris,
was the theatre of the elegances and the home of
pleasant mirthfulness, the appearance of the young
artist at this theatre was in itself an event. But expectations such as these are as perilous to weak pretensions as they are encouraging to real talent ; and if
Charles Mathews triumphed it was in virtue of very
undeniable qualities. Anything so airy and fascinat-
ing as this young man had not been seen upon our
stage. In general, theatres feel that the *jeune premier*
is their weak point. He is bad enough in fiction ;
but in fiction we do not *see* him, whereas on the
stage the weakness of the character is usually aggra-
vated by a "bend in the back" and an implacable
fatuity.

It is a rare assemblage of qualities that enables an
actor to be sufficiently good-looking without being in-
sufferably conceited, to be quiet without being ab-

surdly insignificant, to be lively without being vulgar, to look like a gentleman, to speak and move like a gentleman, and yet to be as interesting as if this quietness were only the restraint of power, not the absence of individuality. And the more pronounced the individuality, that is, the more vivacious the character represented, the greater is the danger of becoming offensive by exaggeration and coarseness.

Charles Mathews was eminently vivacious: a nimble spirit of mirth sparkled in his eye, and gave airiness to every gesture. He was in incessant movement without ever becoming obtrusive or fidgety. A certain grace tempered his vivacity; an innate sense of elegance rescued him from the exaggerations of animal spirits. " He wanted weight," as an old playgoer once reproachfully said of him; but he had the qualities of his defects, and the want of weight became delightful airiness. Whether he danced the Tarentella with charming Miss Fitzpatrick, or snatched up a guitar and sang, he neither danced like a dancer, nor sang like a singer, but threw the charm of a lively nature into both. I think I see him now in " One Hour " seated opposite Madame Vestris, and made to subdue his restless impatience while he held her skeins of silk — a *very* drawing-room version of Hercules at the feet of Omphale—and I picture to myself how the majority of *jeunes premiers* would comport themselves in that position!

In our juvenile apprehensions he was the beau-ideal of elegance. We studied his costumes with ardent devotion. We envied him his tailor, and "made him our patron to live and to die." We could see no faults in him; and all the criticisms which our elders passed on him grated harshly in our ears as the croaking of "fogies." As a proof of my enthusiasm I may mention that I wrote a one-act comedy for him, at an age when anything less than five acts and blank verse seemed beneath the dignity of an aspiring author. (I will do him the justice to say that he did not accept it.)

But if no faults were discernible then, I now see, in retrospect, that it was the charm of the man rather than any peculiar talent in the actor which carried him so successfully through those little Olympic pieces; and that when he began to try his powers in more exacting parts—such as Charles Surface, for instance—there was still the old elegance, but not the old success. Practice and study, however, made him an accomplished comedian within a certain range, the limits of which are determined by his singular want of passionate expression. No good actor I have ever seen was so utterly powerless in the manifestation of all the powerful emotions: rage, scorn, pathos, dignity, vindictiveness, tenderness, and wild mirth are all beyond his means. He cannot even laugh with animal heartiness. He sparkles, he never explodes. Yet his keen observation, his powers of imitation, and a certain artistic power of preserving the unity of a character in all its details, are singularly shown in such parts as Lavater, Sir Charles Coldstream, Mr. Affable Hawk, and the villain in " The Day of Reckoning."

This last mentioned part was, unfortunately for him, excluded from his habitual repertory by the disagreeable nature of the piece. A French melodrama, never worth much even on the Boulevards, and still less adapted to the Lyceum audiences, afforded him an opportunity which I think is unique in his varied career, the opportunity of portraying a melodramatic villain: and he showed himself a great comedian in the way he portrayed it. Imagine a Count D'Orsay destitute alike of principle and of feeling, the incarnation of heartless elegance, cool yet agreeable, admirable in all the externals which make men admired in society, and hateful in all the qualities tested by the serious trials of life; such was the Count presented by Charles Mathews. Instead of "looking the villain," he looked like the man to whom all drawing-rooms would be flung open. Instead of warning away his victims by a countenance and manner more significant of villainy than the description of the " Hue and Cry," he allured them with the graceful ease of a conscience quite at rest, and the manner of an assured acceptance.   Whether the pit really understood this presentation, and felt it as a rare specimen of art, I cannot say; but I am sure that no critic capable of ridding himself of conventional prepossession would see such a bit of action and forget it.

It is needless to speak of his performance in " The Game of Speculation," the artistic merit of which was so great that it almost became an offence against morality, by investing a swindler with irresistible charms, and making the very audacity of deceit a source of pleasurable sympathy. Enough to say that all who had the opportunity of comparing this performance with that of the original actor of the part in France, declared that the superiority of Charles

Mathews was incalculable. (I have since seen Got, the great comedian of the Théâtre Français, in this part, yet I prefer Charles Mathews.)

The multitude of characters, some of them excellent types, which he has portrayed, is so great that I cannot name a third of them. They had all one inestimable quality, that of being pleasant; and the consequence is that he is an universal favorite. Indeed, the personal regard which the public feels for him is something extraordinary when we consider that it is not within the scope of his powers to *move* us by kindling any of our deeper sympathies. And it is interesting to compare this feeling of regard with its absence in the case of Farren. Farren was assuredly a finer actor, and held a more undisputed position on the stage, for he had simply no rival at all. His career was long, and unvaryingly successful. Yet the public which applauded him as an actor did not feel much personal regard for him as a man; whereas for Charles Mathews the feeling was not inaptly expressed by an elderly gentleman in the boxes of the Lyceum on the fall of the curtain one night after "The Game of Speculation": "And to think of such a man being in difficulties! There ought to be a public subscription got up to pay his debts."

———

The reappearance of Charles Mathews in one of his favorite parts, in "Used Up," after having played that part with great success in Paris, naturally attracts large audiences to the Haymarket; and as I had not seen him play it for many years it drew me there, that I might enjoy what now becomes more and more of a rarity, a really fine bit of acting. Nor was my enjoyment balked, as far as he was concerned, although it would have been greater had there been a little more attention paid to the mounting of the piece. The Haymarket Theatre is, or rather pretends to be, our leading theatre for comedy. And on such a stage, or indeed on any stage, the insolent disregard of all artistic conditions which could permit such a performance as that of Sir Adonis Leech by Mr. Rogers (an actor not without merit in certain characters), and which could allow a valet to be dressed like Mr. Clark, implies a state of facile acquiescence on the part of the public which explains the utter decay of the drama. As long as critics are silent and the groundlings laugh, such things will continue. If Mr. Rogers can be accepted as the representative of an English gentleman of our day, if aspect and bearing such as his can pass without protest, what can be the peculiar delight received from the exquisite elegance and verisimilitude of Charles Mathews? My private conviction is that the majority of the audience enjoyed the fun of the *part* with very little enjoyment of the *acting;* and what deepens this conviction is that there was more applause in the second act, where the fun "grows fast and furious," and where the acting is indifferent, than in the first act, where the acting is perfect and the fun mild. As the languorous man of fashion Charles Mathews is faultless. There is an exquisite moderation in his performance

which shows a nice perception of nature. The coolness is never overdone. The languor is never
obtruded. When the blacksmith is threatening him,
there is nothing to suggest that he is assuming an attitude of indifference. From first to last we have a
character the integrity of which is never sacrified to
isolated effects.

But in the second act, where the man of fashion
appears as a plough-boy, all sense of artistic truth is
wanting. There are two methods of carrying out the
dramatic conception of this act—one which should
present a plough-boy, with enough verisimilitude to
deceive the farmer and delight the audience; the
other, which should present a gentleman acting the
plough-boy, and every now and then overacting or
forgetting the part, and always when alone, or with
Mary, relapsing into his native manner. Now Charles
Mathews misses both these. He is not at all like a
plough-boy, nor like Sir Charles Coldstream acting the
plough-boy. So little regard has he to truth, that he
does not even remove the rings from his white fin-
gers, although a jeweled hand is not usually seen
directing a plough. Nor when the farmer is absent
does the removal of such a constraint make any
change in his voice and bearing. The situations of
this act are funny, and the amused spectators perhaps
enjoy the broad contrast between the elegance of Sir
Charles and the homeliness of the plough-boy; but an
accomplished comedian like Charles Mathews ought
to have seized such an opportunity of revealing the
elegance and refined coolness of the man under the
necessary coarseness of his assumed character. The

alternations are just the sort of effects which one could fancy must be tempting to an artist conscious of his powers. It is, however, plain to anyone who is sufficiently critical to discriminate between the acting and the situation, that Charles Mathews has no distinct conception in his mind of any character at all placed in this difficult situation, but that he abandons himself to the situation, and allows the fun of it to do his work. In other words it is farce, not comedy: whereas the first act is comedy, and high comedy.

As I did not see what the French critics wrote about his performance, I cannot say what effect this act had on them. And, indeed, as, according to my experience, the French critics usually confine their remarks to the general impression of a performance, and seldom analyse it, they may have contented themselves with eulogies varied by allusions to Arnal, who created the part. Yet I am much mistaken if they also did not perceive the glaring discrepancy between the first and second acts; and whatever Arnal may have done, I feel persuaded that Bouffé or Got (supposing them to have played the parts) could have made the second act quite as remarkable for its representation of character as the first act.

After " Used Up" came the burlesque of " The Golden Fleece," with Compton delightfully humorous as the King, and Charles Mathews inimitably easy as the Chorus. Compton's burlesque seems to me in the very finest spirit of artistic drollery, and as unlike what is usually attempted as true comedy is unlike efforts to be funny. Bad actors seem to imagine that they have only to be extravagant to be burlesque;

as bad comedians think they have only to make grimaces to be comic. But Robson and Compton, guided
by a true artistic sense, show that burlesque acting is
the grotesque personation of a character, not the outrageous defiance of all character; the personation
has truth, although the character itself may be
preposterously drawn.

A similar remark may be made of the acting of
Charles Mathews as the Chorus. He is assuredly not
what would be called a burlesque actor in the ordinary acceptation of the term, nor would any one
familiar with his style suppose him capable of the
heartiness and force usually demanded by burlesque;
and yet, because he is a fine actor, he is fine also in
burlesque, giving a truthful and easy personation to
an absurd conception. Another actor in such a part
as Chorus would have "gagged" or made grimaces,
would have been extravagant and sought to startle
the public into laughter at broad incongruities.
Charles Mathews is as quiet, easy, elegant, as free
from points and as delightfully humorous as if the
part he played and the words he uttered belonged to
high comedy; he allows the incongruity of the character and the language to work their own laughable
way, and he presents them with the gravity of one
who believed them. Notice also the singular unob-
trusiveness of his manner, even when the situation is
most broadly sketched. For example, when the
King interrupts his song by an appeal to Chorus,
Charles Mathews steps forward, and, bending over
the footlights with that quiet gravity which has hitherto marked his familiar explanations of what is going

on, begins to sing *fol de riddle lol.* There is not one actor in a score who would not have spoiled the humor of this by a wink or grimace at the audience, as much as to say, "Now I'm going to make you laugh." The imperturbable gravity and familiar ease of Mathews give a drollery to this " fol de riddle lol" which is indescribable. Probably few who saw Charles Mathews play the Chorus consider there was any art required so to play it; they can understand that to sing patter songs as he sings them may not be easy, but to be quiet and graceful and humorous, to make every line tell, and yet never show the stress of effort, will not seem wonderful. If they could see another actor in the part it would open their eyes.

CHAPTER VII.

FRÉDÉRIC LEMAÎTRE.

AMONG the few actors of exceptional genius who, by reason of their very individuality, defy clas-sification, and provoke the most contradictory judg-ments, must be placed the singularly gifted Frédéric Lemaître. Those who have only seen him in the pitiable decay of his later years cannot easily under-stand the enthusiasm he excited in his prime; but they will understand it, perhaps, if they reflect that because he was an actor of genius, and not an actor of talent, he necessarily lost his hold of audiences when age and reckless habits had destroyed the per-sonal qualifications which had been the sources of his triumph.

There was always something offensive to good taste in Frédéric's acting—a note of vulgarity, partly owing to his daring animal spirits, but mainly owing, I sus-pect, to an innate vulgarity of nature. In his great moments he was great; but he was seldom admira-ble throughout an entire scene, and never throughout an entire play. In his famous character of Robert Macaire the defects were scarcely felt, because the colossal buffoonery of that conception carried you at once into the region of hyperbole and Aristophanic fun which soared beyond the range of criticism. It disgusted or subdued you at once. In every sense of the word it was a creation. A common melodrama without novelty or point became in his hands a grandiose symbolical caricature; and Robert Macaire became a type, just as Lord Dundreary has become one in our own day. The costume he invented for that part was in itself a magnificent effrontery. It struck the key-note; and as the piece proceeded all was felt to be in harmony with that picture of ideal blackguardism. For the peculiarity of Robert Macaire is the union of a certain ideal grace and *bonhomie* with the most degraded ruffianism and hardness, as of a nobleman preserving some of the instincts and habits of his class amid the instincts and habits of the galleys and the pothouse. If he danced, it was not until he had first pulled on a pair of hyperbolically tattered kid gloves; and while waltzing with incomparable elegance he could not resist picking the pocket of his fair partner. He sang, took snuff, philosophized, and jested with an air of native superiority, and yet made you feel that he was a hateful scoundrel all the while. You laughed at his impudence, you admired his ease and readiness, and yet you would have killed him like a rat. He was jovial, graceful, false, and cruel.

In Don César de Bazan there was another and a very different portrait of the picturesque blackguard. Here also was the union of grace and tatters, of elegance and low habits. The Spanish nobleman had stained his ermine, and dragged his honor through the wine-shop and the brothel; but he had never wholly lost himself, and had not perverted his original nature. It was difficult to conceive anything more disreputable and *débraillé* than this Don César when he first appeared, tipsy and moralizing on the fact that he had "gambled with blackguards, who had cheated him like gentlemen." There was immense exaggeration, but it was the exaggeration of great scene-painting. Very shortly you perceived the real nature of the man underneath—the nature stained, not spoiled, by reckless dissipation; and it was therefore no surprise when, as the play proceeded, the nobler elements of this nature asserted themselves, and Don César claimed respect.

But although Frédéric's performance of this part was in many respects incomparable, it had many serious defects. His love of "gagging" and his subordination of the scene to some particular effect were unpleasantly shown in that capital interview with the king, when his majesty is discovered by Don César in his wife's apartment. He quite spoiled by vulgarity the effect of his retort when the king, not knowing him, gives himself out as Don César. "Vous êtes Don César de Bazan? Eh bien! alors je suis le Roi d'Espagne." He made it very comical, but it was farcical and inartistic; and the stupid appeal to the vulgarest laughter of the audience in the grotesquely extravagant feather which danced in his hat was suited to a pantomime or burlesque, but very unsuited to the serious situation of the drama.

Very different was his acting in the prison scene, and especially noticeable was the rapid change from jovial conviviality over the wine cup to serious and dignified attention while the sentence of death was being passed on him. He stood with the napkin carelessly thrown over his arm, his hand lightly resting on one hip, and listened with grave calmness to the sentence; at its conclusion he relapsed into the convivial mood, exclaiming, " Troisième couplet !" as he resumed his song; and you felt the irony of his gravity, felt the unutterable levity of his nature.

In pathos of a domestic kind, and in outbursts of passion, Lemaître was singularly affecting. When he played in " Paillasse," " Trente Ans de la Vie d'un Joueur," and " La Dame de St. Tropez," he left indelible impressions of pathos and of lurid power; but I must confess that I not only thought very little of his " Ruy Blas," but always doubted whether his style of acting were not essentially unsuited to the poetic drama. He seemed to feel himself ill at ease, walking upon stilts. His expressions were conventional, and his gestures vehement and often common. As the lackey he was ignoble ; as the minister and lover his declamation was, to my thinking, cold and unimpassioned in its violence. This, however, was not the opinion of M. Victor Hugo, who, as a Frenchman and the author of the play, may be supposed to be a better judge than I am, and in fairness I will quote what he says in the appendix to his play: " Quant à M. Frédéric Lemaître, qu'en dire ? Les acclamations enthousiastes de la foule le saississent à son entrée en scéne [rather premature enthusiasm] et le suivent jusqu'après le dénouement. Rêveur et profond au premier acte, mélancolique au deuxième, grand, passionné, et sublime au troisième, il s'élève au cinquième à l'un de ses prodigieux effets tragiques du haut desquels l'acteur rayonnant domine tous les souvenirs de son art. Pour les vieillards c'est Lekain et Garrick mêlés dans un seul homme ; pour nous c'est l'action de Kean combinée avec l'émotion de Talma. Et pius, partout, à travers les éclairs éblouissants de son jeu, M. Frédéric a des larmes, de ces vraies larmes qui font pleurer les autres, de ces larmes dont parle Horace : *si vis me flere dolendum est primum ipsi tibi.*"

In answer to such a dithyramb as this I can only appeal to the recollections of those readers who have seen Frédéric play Ruy Blas. For myself I confess to have the smallest possible pleasure in a French actor when he is "profond et rêveur;" and that not only did I detect no tears in Frédéric's Ruy Blas, but his sublime tragic effects—what the French critics call " ses explosions "—left me wholly unmoved. Indeed, to speak of Lemaître as a rival of Kean or Rachel seems to me like comparing Eugène Sue with Victor Hugo—the gulf that separates prose from poetry yawns between them.

Lemaître was very handsome. He had a wonderful eye, with large orbit, a delicate and sensitive mouth, a fine nose, a bold jaw, a figure singularly graceful, and a voice penetrating and sympathetic. He had great animal spirits, great daring, great fancy, and great energy of animal passion. He always created his parts—that is to say, gave them a specific stamp of individuality; and the creative activity of his imagination was seen in a hundred novel details.

But as his physical powers decayed his acting became less and less effective; for in losing the personal charm, it had no stage traditions to fall back upon. And the last time I saw him, which must be fourteen or fifteen years ago, he was rapidly degenerating, every now and then a flash of the old fire would be visible, but the effects were vanishing and the defects increasing. An interesting letter which recently appeared in the *Pall Mall Gazette* gave a graphic account of this great actor in the last stages of his ruin. I should be sorry to see the man who had once swayed audiences with irresistible power reduced to the painful feebleness which this correspondent describes.

CHAPTER VIII.

THE TWO KEELEYS.

AMONG my very pleasantest recollections of the stage arise the figures of Keeley and his wife, each standing alone as a type of comic acting, and each markedly illustrating the truth so little understood, that acting, because it is a *representative* art, cannot be created by intelligence or sensibility (however necessary these may be for the perfection of the art), but must always depend upon the physical qualifications of the actor, these being the means of representation. It matters little what the actor *feels;* what he can *express* gives him his distinctive value.

Keeley was undoubtedly equipped with unusual advantages, over and above his intelligence. His handsome, pleasant features set in a large fat face, his beetling brow and twinkling eye, his rotund little body, neither ungraceful nor inactive, at once prepossessed the spectator; and his unctuous voice and laugh completed the conquest. He was drollery personified : drollery without caricature, drollery without ugliness, drollery that had an *arrière pensée* of cleverness, and nothing of harshness or extravagance. To define him by a comparison, he was a duodecimo Falstaff.

Mrs. Keeley had little or none of the unctuousness of her husband, but she also was remarkably endowed. She was as intense and pointed as he was easy and fluent. She concentrated into her repartees an amount of intellectual *vis* and "devil" which gave such a feather to the shaft that authors must often have been surprised at the revelation to themselves of the force of their own wit. Eye, voice, gesture sparkled and chuckled. You could see that she enjoyed the joke, but enjoyed it rather as an intellectual triumph over others, than (as in Keeley's case) from an impersonal delight in the joke itself. Keeley was like a fat, happy, self-satisfied puppy, taking life easily, ready to get sniffing and enjoyment out of everything. Mrs. Keeley was like a sprightly kitten, eager to make a mouse of every moving thing.

The humorous predominated in Keeley; in his wife the predominant mood was self-assertion: so that the one was naturally the comic servant, the other the pert soubrette. The one took kindly to his vices; he was a glutton, a liar, a coward, was kicked and bullied, and bemoaned his lot without ever forfeiting our good-will. He never made a pretense of virtue; he threw all his vices on his organization: if blame had to be pronounced Nature must bear it. He was never despicable; even in the moments of abject terror (and no one could represent comic terror better than he did) somehow or other he contrived to make you feel that courage ought not to be expected of him, for cowardice was simply the natural trembling of that human jelly. He lied with a grace which made it a sort of truth—a personal and private truth. He chuckled over his sensuality in such an unsuspiciousness of moral candor, and with such an intensity of relish, that you almost envied his gulosity. He was, in fact, a great idealist.

When people foolishly objected that he was "always Keeley," they forgot in the first place that an actor with so peculiar an organization could not disguise his individuality; and in the second place, that in spite of the familiar face, voice, and manner which necessarily reappeared under all disguises, the representative power of the actor did really display itself in very various types. Keeley played many parts, and played them variously. No one who had seen his Sir Andrew Aguecheek could detect in it traces of Waddilove (in "To Parents and Guardians"); no one who had laughed at his Acres could recognize it in "Two o'Clock in the Morning;" no one who had enjoyed his terror in "A Thumping Legacy" could recognize the same type in " Box and Cox." In fact, the range of his creations was unusually wide, and I do not remember to have seen him absolutely fail to represent the character, except in the single instance of Sir Hugh Evans, a part from which he was intellectually and physically excluded—the irritable, irascible, lean, pedantic Welsh parson being the very last kind of character which his representative powers could express.

It was not said of Mrs. Keeley that she was "always Mrs. Keeley," although in truth her strongly marked peculiarities were quite incapable of disguise; but she laid hold of some characteristic in the part she was playing, and rendered it with such sharpness of outline and such force of effect that her own individuality was lost sight of to the uncritical eye. Her physique was also more flexible than that of her husband, and she could "make up" better. Her perception of characteristics (within a certain range) was very acute ; and sometimes she presented a character with extraordinary felicity. Did the reader happen to see her play the maid of all work in "Furnished Apartments"? He will not easily forget such a picture of the London "slavey," a stupid, wearied, slatternly good-natured dab, her brain confused by incessant bells, her vitality ebbing under overwork. He will not forget the dazed expression, the limp exhaustion of her limbs, or the wonderful assemblage of rags which passed for her costume. There was something at once inexpressibly droll and pathetic in this picture. It was so grotesque, yet so real, that laughter ended in a sigh.

In quite a different style was her performance of Bob Nettles (in "To Parents and Guardians"), the only representation of a masculine character by a woman that I remember to have seen with perfect satisfaction. She was the school-boy in every look and gesture.

It should be noted that whereas Keeley was eminently an idealist, and as capable of personating characters in high and poetic comedy as in broad farce, Mrs. Keeley was eminently a realist, and her realism was always a disturbing tendency in poetic comedy. To see the two as Audrey and Touchstone was indeed to see acting the like of which has rarely been seen since ; but her Audrey, though mirth-provoking, belonged altogether to another region of art than that of Keeley's Touchstone. In the first place, it was unpoetic; in the second place, it was defective in that the stupidity was conscious stupidity —the mask of a sharp, keen face, not the stolidity of a country wench. When Keeley played Sir Andrew Aguecheek you had no suspicion of a keen, clear intellect lurking behind that fatuity; you felt that beef does harm the wit, and that he had been a great eater of beef. But when Mrs. Keeley's Audrey asks, "What is poetry? is it a true thing?" you heard in her accent, and saw in her eye, that she knew more about the matter than Touchstone himself.

Keeley could play a gentleman; Mrs. Keeley could never rise above the servants' hall. But, on the other hand, Mrs. Keeley had a power over the more energetic passions which he wanted; she was an excellent melodramatic actress, and her pathos drew tears.

In Jerrold's capital little piece, "The Prisoners of War,' Keeley and his wife were seen to great advantage. As the vulgar, bragging Englishman, despising Frenchmen and everything French because it was not Cockney, his idealism preserved the real comedy of the type from degenerating into gross caricature or unpleasant truthfulness. One recognized the national failing; but one liked the good-natured Briton. To hear him haughtily wave aside the objection to the taxes in England: "Taxes! We haven't the word in our language. There are two or three duties, to be sure" (this was said with a mild candor, admitting what could not be of the slightest consequence): "but" (and here the buoyant confidence of superiority once more reappeared in his accent) "with us duties are pleasures." (And then following up with a hyperbole of assurance) "As for taxes, you'd make an Englishman stare only to mention such things." Not less amusing was his defence when reproached for this bragging:

Pall Mall.—As a sailor, isn't it your duty to die for your country? *Firebrace.*—Most certainly. *Pall Mall.*—*As a civilian it is mine to lie for her.* Courage isn't confined to fighting.   No, no ; whenever a Frenchman throws me down a lie, for the honor of England I always trump it.

The convincing logic of this used to set the house in a roar.   But it was his manner which gave the joke its *bouquet;* and when he vindicated the superiority of the air of England over the air of France, on the ground that " it goes twice as far—it's twice as thick," the pit screamed with delight.   Mrs. Keeley as Polly Pall Mall had an inferior part, but by her make-up, and, above all, by the inimitable manner in which she read a letter interrupted by sobs, she raised the part into first-rate importance.

It is an inestimable loss our stage has suffered by the departure of two such actors.   Keeley was equally at home in broad farce, high comedy, and ideal scenes, always an idealist, always true, always humorous. Mrs. Keeley was great in farce, low comedy, and melodrama, pathetic and humorous, and always closely imitative of daily life.   Their career was one uninterrupted triumph, and they live in the memory of play-goers with a halo of personal affection round their heads.

CHAPTER IX.

SHAKSPEARE AS ACTOR AND CRITIC.

SHAKSPEARE was most probably an indifferent actor. If a doubt is permissible on this point, there is none respecting his mastery as a critic. He may not have been a brilliant executant; he was certainly a penetrating and reflective connoisseur.

Modern idolaters, who cannot see faults in Shakpeare's plays which are still before us, and which to unbiased eyes present defects both numerous and glaring, may perhaps consider it an impertinence to infer any defects in his acting, which is not before us, which has long ceased to be remembered, and which never seems to have been much spoken of. Why not, with a generous enthusiasm, assume that it was fine? Why not suppose that the creator of so many living, breathing characters must have been also a noble personator? There is nothing to prevent the generous admirer indulging in this hypothesis if he finds comfort in it. I merely remark that it has no evidence in its favor, and a great many points against it. The mere fact that we hear nothing of his qualities as an actor implies that there was nothing above the line, nothing memorable, to be spoken of. We hear of him as wit and companion, as poet and man of business, but not a word of his qualities as an actor. Of Burbage, Alleyn, Tarleton, Knell, Bentley, Miles, Wilson, Crosse, Pope, and others, we hear more or less; but all that tradition vaguely wafts to us of Shakspeare is, that he played the Ghost in " Hamlet," and Old Knowell in " Everv Man in His Humor," neither of them parts wnich demand or admit various excellences.

Like many other dramatists of the early time— Munday, Chettle, Lodge, Kyd, Nash, Ben Jonson, Heywood, Dekker, and Rowley—he adopted sock and buskin as a means of making money; and it is probable that, like actors of all times, he had a favorable opinion of his own performances. He certainly was able to see through the tricks and devices with which more popular players captivated " the groundlings," and was doubtless one of the " judicious " whom these devices grieved. But in spite of his marvellous genius, in spite of the large flexibility of mind which could enable him to conceive great varieties of character, it is highly probable that he wanted the mimetic flexibility of organization which could alone have enabled him to *personate* what he conceived. The powers of conception and the powers of presentation are distinct. A poet is rarely a good reader of his own verse, and has never yet been a great personator of his own characters. Shakspeare doubtless knew— none knew so well—how Hamlet, Othello, Richard, and Falstaff should be personated; but had he been called upon to personate them he would have found himself wanting in voice, face, and temperament.

The delicate sensitiveness of his organization, which is implied in the exquisiteness and flexibility of his genius, would absolutely have unfitted him for the presentation of characters demanding a robust vigor and a weighty animalism. It is a vain attempt to paint frescoes with a camel's-hair brush. The broad and massive effects necessary to scenic presentation could never have been produced by such a temperament as his. Thus even on the supposition of his having been a good drawing-room mime, he would have wanted the qualities of a good actor. And we have no ground for inferring that he was even a good drawing-room mime.

I dare say he declaimed finely, as far as rhythmic cadence and a nice accentuation went. But his non-success implies that his voice was intractable, or limited in its range. Without a sympathetic voice, no declamation can be effective. The tones which stir us need not be musical, need not be pleasant even, but they must have a penetrating, vibrating quality. Had Shakspeare possessed such a voice he would have been famous as an actor. Without it all his other gifts were as nothing on the stage. Had he seen Garrick, Kemble, or Kean performing in plays not his own he might doubtless have perceived a thousand deficiencies in their conception, and defects in their execution; but had he appeared on the same stage with them, even in plays of his own, the audiences would have seen the wide gulf between conception and presentation. One lurid look, one pathetic intonation, would have more power in swaying the emotions of the audience than all the subtle and profound passion which agitated the soul of the poet, but did not manifestly express itself : the look and the tone may come from a man so drunk as to be scarcely able to stand ; but the public sees only tne look, hears only the tone, and is irresistibly moved by these intelligible symbols.

That Shakspeare, as a critic, had mastered the principles of the art of acting is apparent from the brief but pregnant advice to the players in " Hamlet." He first insists on the necessity of a flexible elocution. He gives no rules for the management of voice and accent ; but in his emphatic warning against the common error of " mouthing," and his request to have the speech spoken " trippingly on the tongue," it is easy to perceive what he means. The word " trippingly," to modern ears, is not perhaps felicitously descriptive ; but the context shows that it indicates easy naturalness as opposed to artificial mouthing. It is further enforced by the advice as to gesture : " Do not saw the air too much with your hand, but use all gently."

After the management of the voice, actors most err in the management of the body : they mouth their sentences, and emphasize their gestures, iri the effort to be effective, and in ignorance of the psychological conditions on which effects depend. In each case the effort to aggrandize natural expression leads to exaggeration and want of truth. In attempting the ideal they pass into the artificial. The tones and gestures of ordinary unimpassioned moments would not, they feel, be appropriate to ideal characters and impassioned situations ; and the difficulty of the art lies precisely in the selection of idealized expressions which shall, to the spectator, be symbols of real emotions. All but very great actors are redundant in gesticulation; not simply overdoing the significant, but unable to repress insignificant movements. Shakspeare must have daily seen this; and therefore he bids the actor " suit the action to the word, with this special observance, that you overstep not the modesty of nature; for anything so overdone is from the purpose of playing, whose end, both at first and now, was and is to hold, as it were, the mirror up to nature.")

It would be worth the actor's while to borrow a hint from the story of Voltaire's pupil, when, to repress her tendency towards exuberant gesticulation, he ordered her to rehearse with her hands tied to her side. She began her recitation in this enforced quietness, but at last, carried away by the movement of her feelings, she flung up her arms, and snapped the threads. In tremor she began to apologize to the poet; he, smiling, reassured her that the gesticulation was *then* admirable, because it was irrepressible. If actors will study fine models they will learn that gestures, to be effective, must be significant, and to be significant they must be rare. To stand still on the stage (and not appear a guy) is one of the elementary difficulties of the art—and one which is rarely mastered.

Having indicated his views on declamation, Shakspeare proceeds to utter golden advice on expression. He specially warns the actor against both over-vehemence and coldness. Remembering that the actor

is an artist, he insists on the observance of that cardinal principle in all art the subordination of impulse
to law, the regulation of all effects with a view to
beauty. "In the very torrent, tempest, and, as I may
say, whirlwind of passion, you must acquire and be-
get a temperance that may give it smoothness. O!
it offends me to the soul to hear a robustious peri-
wig-pated fellow tear a passion to tatters, to very
rags, to split the ears of the groundlings." What is
this but a recognition of the mastery of art, by
which the ruling and creating intellect makes use of
passionate symbols, and subordinates them to a
pleasurable end? If the actor were really in a passion his voice would be a scream, his gestures wild
and disorderly; he would present a painful, not an
æsthetic spectacle. He must therefore select from
out the variety of passionate expressions only those
that can be harmoniously subordinated to a general
whole. (He must be at once passionate and temper-
ate: trembling with emotion, yet with a mind in
vigilant supremacy controlling expression, *directing*
every intonation, look and gesture. The rarity of
fine acting depends on the difficulty there is in being
at one and the same moment so deeply moved that
the emotion shall spontaneously express itself in
symbols universally intelligible, and yet so calm as to
be perfect master of effects, capable of modulating
voice and moderating gesture when they tend to
excess or ugliness.

"To preserve this medium between mouthing and
meaning too little," says Colley Cibber, "to keep the
attention more pleasingly awake by a tempered spirit

than by mere vehemence of voice, is of all the master
strokes of an actor the most difficult to reach." Some
critics, annoyed by rant, complain of the ranter being
"too fiery." As Lessing says, an actor cannot have
too much fire, but he may easily have too little
sense. Vehemence without real emotion is rant;
vehemence with real emotion, but without art, is turbulence. To be loud and exaggerated is the easy
resource of actors who have no faculty; to be vehement and agitated is to betray the inexperience of one
who has not yet mastered the art. "Be not too tame
neither," Shakspeare quickly adds, lest his advice
should be misunderstood, "but let your own discretion be your tutor." Yes; the actor's discretion must
tell him when he has hit upon the right tone and
right expression, which must first be suggested to
him by his own feelings. In endeavoring to express
emotions, he will try various tones, various gestures,
various accelerations and retardations of the rhythm;
and during this tentative process his vigilant discretion will arrest those that are effective, and discard
the rest.

It is because few actors are sufficiently reflective
that good acting is so rare; and the tameness of a
few who are reflective, but not passionate, brings dis-
credit on reflection. Such study as actors mostly give
is to imitation of others, rather than to introspection
of their own means; and this is fatal to excellence.
"Nous devons être sensibles," said Talma once;
"nous devons éprouver l'émotion; mais pour mieux
l'imiter, pour mieux en saisir les caractères par l'étude
et la réflexion."

The anecdotes about Macready and Liston given on page 44 suggest a topic of some interest in relation to the art of acting: In how far does the actor feel the emotion he expresses? When we hear of Macready and Liston lashing themselves into a fury behind the scenes in order to come on the stage sufficiently excited to give a truthful representation of the agitations of anger, the natural inference is that these artists recognized the truth of the popular notion which assumes that the actor really feels what he expresses. But this inference seems contradicted by experience. Not only is it notorious that the actor is feigning, and that if he really felt what he feigns he would be unable to withstand the wear and tear of such emotion repeated night after night; but it is indisputable (to those who know anything of art, that the mere presence of genuine emotion would be such a disturbance of the intellectual equilibrium as entirely to frustrate artistic expression.) Talma told M. Barrière that he was once carried away by the truth and beauty of the actress playing with him till she recalled him by a whisper: "Take care, Talma, you are moved!" on which he remarked, "C'est qu'en effet de l'émotion naît le trouble: la voix résiste, la mémoire manque, les gestes sont faux, l'effet est detruit;" and there is an observation of Molé to a similar effect: "Je ne suis pas content de moi ce soir; je me suis trop livré, je ne suis pas resté mon maître: j'étais entré trop vivement dans la situation; j'étais le personnage même, je n'étais plus l'acteur qui le joue. J'ai été vrai comme je le serais

chez moi; *pour l'optique du théâtre il faut l'être
autrement.*"

Everyone initiated into the secrets of the art of
acting will seize at once the meaning of this luminous
phrase *l'optique du théâtre;* and the uninitiated will understand how entirely opposed to all the purposes of
art and all the secrets of effect would be the representation of passion in its *real* rather than in its *symbolical* expression : the red, swollen, and distorted features of grief, the harsh and screaming intonation of
anger, are unsuited to art ; the paralysis of all outward expression, and the flurry and agitation of ungraceful gesticulation which belong to certain
powerful emotions, may be described by the poet,
but cannot be admitted into plastic art. The poet
may tell us what is signified by the withdrawal of all
life and movement from the face and limbs, describing the internal agitations or the deadly calm which
disturb or paralyze the sufferer; but the painter,
sculptor, or actor must tell us what the sufferer un-
dergoes, and tell it through the symbols of outward
expression—the internal workings must be legible in
the external symbols; and these external symbols
must also have a certain grace and proportion to
affect us æsthetically.

(All art is symbolical.) If it presented emotion in
its real expression it would cease to move us as art ;
sometimes cease to move us at all, or move us only to
laughter. There is a departure from reality in all the
stage accessories. The situation, the character, the
language, all are at variance with daily experience.
Emotion does not utter itself in verse nor in carefully

chosen sentences, and to speak verse with the negli-
gence of prose is a serious fault.   There is a good passage in Colley Cibber s account of Betterton, which
actors, and critics who are not alive to the immense
effects that lie in fine elocution, would do well to pon-
der on.   "In the just delivery of poetical numbers,
particularly where the sentiments are pathetic, it is
scarce credible upon how minute an article of sound
depends their greatest beauty or inaffection.   The
voice of a singer is not more strictly ty'd to time
and tune, than that of an actor in theatrical elocution.   The least syllable too long, or too slightly dwelt
upon in a period, depreciates it to nothing; which
very syllabie, if rightly touched, shall, like the height-
ening stroke of light from a master's pencil, give life
and spirit to the whole."   It is superfluous to insist
on the utter impossibility of attending to such delicate minutiæ if the speaker be really agitated by
emotion.   A similar remark applies to all the other
details of his art. (His looks and gestures, his position in the picture, all will be out of proportion and
fail of their due effect unless he is master of himself.

The reader sees at once that as a matter of fact the
emotions represented by the actor are not agitating
him as they would agitate him in reality; he is feigning and we know that he is feigning; he is representing a fiction which is to move us as a fiction, and not
to lacerate our sympathies as they would be lacerated
by the agony of a fellow-creature actually suffering
in our presence.   The tears we shed are tears welling
from a sympathetic source; but their salt bitterness
is removed, and their pain is pleasurable.

But now arises the antinomy, as Kant would call it—the contradiction which perplexes judgment. If the actor lose all power over his art under the disturbing influence of emotion, he also loses all power over his art in proportion to his deadness to emotion. If he really feel, he cannot act; but he cannot act unless he feel. All the absurd efforts of mouthing and grimacing actors to produce an effect, all the wearisomeness of cold conventional representation— mimicry without life—we know to be owing to the unimpassioned talent of the actor. Observe, I do not say to his unimpassioned nature. It is quite possible for a man of exquisite sensibility to be ludicrously tame in his acting, if he has not the requisite talent of expression, or has not yet learned how to modulate it so as to give it due effect. The other day in noticing the rare ability of Mdle. Lucca in depicting the emotions of Margaret in " Faust," I had occasion to remark on the surprising transformation which had taken place in two years, changing her from a feeble, conventional, ineffective actress into a passionate, subtle, and original artist. In the practice of two years she had learned the secrets of expression; she had learned to modulate; and having learned this, having felt her way, she could venture to give play to the suggestions of her impulses, which before that had doubtless alarmed her. But although it is quite possible for an actor to have sensibility without the talent of expression, and therefore to be a tame actor though an impassioned man, it is wholly impossible for him to express what he has never felt, to be an impassioned actor with a cold nature.

And here is the point of intersection of the two lines of argument just followed out. The condition being that a man must feel emotion if he is to express it, for if he does not feel it he will not know how to express it, how can this be reconciled with the impossibility of his affecting us æsthetically while he is disturbed by emotion? In other words: *how far* does he really feel the passion he expresses? It is a question of degree. As in all art, feeling lies at the root, but the foliage and flowers, though deriving their sap from emotion, derive their form and structure from the intellect. The poet cannot write while his eyes are full of tears, while his nerves are trembling from the mental shock, and his hurrying thoughts are too agitated to settle into definite tracks. But he must have felt, or his verse will be a mere echo. It is from the memory of past feelings that he draws the beautiful image with which he delights us. He is tremulous again under the remembered agitation, but it is a pleasant tremor, and in no way disturbs the clearness of his intellect. He is a spectator of his own tumult; and though moved by it, can yet so master it as to select from it only these elements which suit his purpose. We are all spectators of ourselves; but it is the peculiarity of the artistic nature to indulge in such introspection even in moments of all but the most disturbing passion, and to draw thence materials for art. This is true also of the fine actor, and many of my readers will recognize the truth of what Talma said of himself: "I have suffered cruel losses, and have often been assailed with profound sorrows; but after the first moment when grief vents itself in cries and tears, I have found myself involuntarily turning my gaze inwards ('je faisais un retour sur mes souffrances'), and found that the actor was unconsciously studying the man, and catching nature in the act." It is only by thus familiarizing oneself with the nature of the various emotions, that one can properly interpret them. But even that is not enough. They must be watched in others, the interpreting key being given in our own consciousness. Having something like an intellectual appreciation of the sequences of feeling and their modes of manifestation, the actor has next to select out of these such as his own physical qualifications enable him to reproduce effectively, and such as will be universally intelligible. To quote Talma once more: "Oui, nous devons être sensibles, nous devons éprouver l'émotion; mais pour mieux l'imiter, pour mieux en saisir les caractères par l'étude et la réflexion. Notre art en exige de profonds. Point d'improvisation possible sur la scéne sous peine d'échec. Tout est calculé, tout doit être prévu, et l'émotion qui semble soudaine, et le trouble qui paraîtd involontaire. L'intonation, le geste, le regard qui semblent inspirés, ont été répétés cent fois."

All this I may assume the reader to accept without dissent, and yet anticipate his feeling some perplexity in reconciling it with the anecdotes which started this digression. Surely, he may say, neither Macready nor Liston could have been so unfamiliar with rage and its manifestations that any hesitation could paralyze their efforts to express these. Why then this preparation behind the scenes? Simply because it was absolutely necessary that they should be in a state of excitement if they were to represent it with truthfulness; and having temperaments which were not instantaneously excitable by the mere imagination of a scene, they prepared themselves. Actors like Edmund Kean, Rachel, or Lemaître found no difficulty in the most rapid transitions; they could one moment chat calmly and the next explode. The imaginative sympathy instantaneously called up all the accessories of expression; one tone would send vibrations through them powerful enough to excite the nervous discharge.

The answer to the question, How far does the actor feel? is, therefore, something like this: He is in a state of emotional excitement sufficiently strong to furnish him with the elements of expression, but not strong enough to disturb his consciousness of the fact that he is only imagining—sufficiently strong to give the requisite tone to his voice and aspect to his features, but not strong enough to prevent his modulating the one and arranging the other according to a preconceived standard. His passion must be ideal—sympathetic, not personal. He may hate with a rival's hate the actress to whom he is manifesting tenderness, or love with a husband's love the actress to whom he is expressing vindictiveness; but for Juliet or Desdemona he must feel love and wrath. One day Malibran, upbraiding Templeton for his coldness towards her in the love scenes of "La Sonnambula," asked him if he were not married, and told him to imagine that she was his wife. The stupid tenor, entirely misunderstanding her, began to be superfluously tender at rehearsal, whereupon she playfully recalled to him that it was during the performance he was to imagine her to be Mrs. Templeton—at rehearsal Mdme. Malibran.

We sometimes hear amateur critics object to fine actors that they are every night the same, never varying their gestures or their tones. This is stigmatized as "mechanical"; and the critics innocently oppose to it some ideal of their own which they call "inspiration." Actors would smile at such nonsense. What is called inspiration is the mere haphazard of carelessness or incompetence; the actor is seeking an expression which he ought to have found when studying his part. What would be thought of a singer who sang his aria differently every night? In the management of his breath, in the distribution of light and shade, in his phrasing, the singer who knows how to sing never varies. The *timbre* of his voice, the energy of his spirit, may vary; but his methods are invariable. Actors learn their parts as singers learn their songs. Every detail is deliberative, or has been deliberated. The very separation of art from nature involves this calculation. The sudden flash of suggestion which is called inspiration may be valuable, it may be worthless: the artistic intellect estimates the value, and adopts or rejects it accordingly.

Trusting to the inspiration of the moment is like trusting to a shipwreck for your first lesson in swimming.

A greater master of the art, practical and theoretical, as actor and teacher, the late M. Sanson, of the Théâtre Français, has well said:

> Méditez, réglez tout, essayez tout d'avance ;
> Un assidu travail donne la confiance.
> L'aisance est du talent le plus aimable attrait :
> *Un jeu bien préparé nous semble sans apprêt.*

And elsewhere:

> Mais, en s'abandonnant, que l'artiste s'observe ;
> De vos heureux hasards sachez vous souvenir :
> Ce qu'il n'a pas produit, l'art doit le retenir,
> L'acteur qui du talent veut atteindre le faîte,
> Quand il livre son cœur doit conserver sa tête.*

Shakspeare, who had learned this in his experience as a dramatist, saw that it was equally true of dramatic representation. The want of calculation in actors distressed him. He saw the public applauding players "who, having neither the accent of Christians, nor the gait of Christian, pagan, nor man, have so strutted and bellowed" that they seemed the products of nature's journeymen. He saw them mistaking violence for passion, turbulence for art, and he bade them remember the purpose of playing, which was to hold the mirror up to nature.

Besides these cardinal directions, Shakspeare gives another which is of minor importance, though it points at a real evil. Avoid gag, he says. It will make some barren spectators laugh, but it shows a pitiful ambition. This, however, is a fault which the

---

* *L'Art Théâtral*, Chant I.—Every studious actor should meditate the counsels of this excellent work.

audience can correct if it please. Generally audiences are so willing to have their laughter excited as to be indifferent to the means employed. Gagging, therefore, is, always was, and always will be popular. I merely allude to it to show how complete is Shakspeare's advice to the players, and how seriously he had considered the whole subject of acting.

CHAPTER X.

ON NATURAL ACTING.

IT has commonly been held to be a dexterous and delicate compliment to Garrick's acting that Fielding has paid through the humorous criticisms of Partridge, who saw nothing admirable in " the terror of the little man," but thought the actor who played the king was deserving of great praise. " He speaks all his words distinctly, half as loud again as the other. Anybody may see he is an actor." I cannot say what truth there was in Partridge's appreciation of Garrick, but if his language is to be interpreted as Fielding seems to imply, the intended compliment is a sarcasm. Partridge says, with a contemptuous sneer, " He the best player! Why, I could act as well as he myself. I am sure if I had seen a ghost, I should have looked in the very same manner, and done just as he did."

Now assuming this to be tolerably near the truth, it implies that Garrick's acting was what is called " natural;" but *not* the natural presentation of a Hamlet. The melancholy, sceptical prince in the presence of his father's ghost must have felt a tremulous and solemn awe, but cannot have felt the vulgar terror of a vulgar nature; yet Partridge says, " If

that little man upon the stage is not frightened, I never saw any man frightened in my life." The manner of a frightened Partridge can never have been at all like the manner of Hamlet. Let us turn to Colley Cibber's remarks on Betterton, if we would see how a great actor represented the emotion: " You have seen a Hamlet, perhaps, who on the first appearance of his father's spirit has thrown himself into all the straining vociferation requisite to express rage and fury, and the house has thundered with applause, though the misguided actor was all the while tearing a passion into rags. I am the more bold to offer you this particular instance because the late Mr. Addison, while I sate by him to see this scene acted, made the same observation, asking me, with some surprise, if I thought Hamlet should be in so violent a passion with the ghost, which, though it might have astonished, it had not provoked him. For you may observe that in this beautiful speech the passion never rises beyond an almost breathless astonishment, or an impatience limited by filial reverence to enquire into the suspected wrongs that may have raised him from his peaceful tomb, and a desire to know what a spirit so seemingly distressed might wish or enjoin a sorrowful son to execute towards his future quiet in the grave. This was the light into which Betterton threw this scene: which he opened with a pause of mute amazement, then slowly rising to a solemn trembling voice he made the ghost equally terrible to the spectator as to himself. And in the descriptive part of the natural emotions which the ghastly visions gave him, the boldness of his expostulation was still governed by

decency, manly but not braving; his voice never
rising to that seeming outrage or wild defiance of
what he naturally revered. But, alas! to preserve
this medium between mouthing and meaning too
little, to keep the attention more pleasingly awake by
a tempered spirit than by mere vehemence of voice,
is of all the master-strokes of an actor the most
difficult to reach."

It is obvious that the naturalness required from
Hamlet is very different from the naturalness of a
Partridge; and Fielding made a great mistake in assimilating the representation of Garrick to the nature
of a serving-man. We are not necessarily to believe
that Garrick made this mistake; but on the showing
of his eulogist he fell into an error quite as reprehen-
sible as the error of the actor who played the king,
and whose stilted declamation was recognized by
Partridge as something like acting. That player had
at least a sense of the *optique du théâtre* which demanded a more elevated style than would have
suited the familiarity of daily intercourse. He knew
he was there to act, to represent a king, to impress
an idealized image on the spectator's mind, and he
could not succeed by the naturalness of his own manner. That he failed in his attempt proves that he
was an imperfect artist; but the attempt was an attempt at art. Garrick (assuming the accuracy of
Fielding's description) failed no less egregiously,
though in a different way. He was afraid of being
stilted, and he relapsed into vulgarity. He tried to
be natural, without duly considering the kind of nature that was to be represented. The supreme diffi-

culty of an actor is to represent ideal character with such truthfulness that it shall affect us as real, not to drag down ideal character to the vulgar level. His art is one of representation, not of illusion. He has to use natural expressions, but he must sublimate them; the symbols must be such as we can sympathetically interpret, and for this purpose they must be the expressions of real human feeling; but just as the language is poetry, or choice prose, purified from the hesitancies, incoherences, and imperfections of careless daily speech, so must his utterance be measured, musical, and incisive—his manner typical and pictorial. If the language depart too widely from the logic of passion and truthfulness, we call it bombast; if the elevation of the actor's style be not sustained by natural feeling, we call it mouthing and rant; and if the language fall below the passion we call it prosaic and flat; as we call the actor tame if he cannot present the character so as to interest us. The most general error of authors, and of actors, is turgidity rather than flatness. The striving to be effective easily leads into the error of exaggeration. But it by no means follows, as some persons seem to imply, that, because exaggeration is a fault, tameness is a merit. Exaggeration is a fault because it is an untruth; but in art it is as easy to be untrue by falling below as by rising above naturalness.

The acting of Mr. Horace Wigan, as the pious banker in "The Settling Day," which suggested these remarks, is quite as much below the truth of nature in its tameness and absence of individuality, as it would have been above the truth had he represented the conventional stage hypocrite. He did not by exaggeration shock our common sense; but neither did he delight our artistic sense by his art. If his performance was without offence, it was also without charm. Some of the audience were doubtless gratified to notice the absence of conventionalism; but I suspect that the majority were tepid in their admiration; and critics would ask whether Mr. Horace Wigan could have given a strongly marked individuality to the character, and at the same time have preserved the ease and naturalness which the representation demanded. Is he not like some novelists, who can be tolerably natural so long as they are creeping on the level of every-day incident and talk, but who become absurdly unnatural the instant they have to rise to the "height of their high argument" either in character or passion? Miss Austen's novels are marvels of art, because they are exquisitely true, and interesting in their truth. Miss Austen's imitators fondly imagine that to be quiet and prosaic—in pages which might as well have been left unwritten —is all that the simplicity of art demands. But in art, simplicity is economy, not meagreness: it is the absence of superfluities, not the suppression of essentials; it arises from an ideal generalization of real and essential qualities, guided by an exquisite sense of proportion.

If we once understand that naturalness in acting means truthful presentation of the character indicated by the author, and not the foisting of commonplace manner on the stage, there will be a ready recognition of each artist's skill, whether he rep-

resent the naturalness of a Falstaff, or the naturalness of a Sir Peter Teazle, or the naturalness of a
Hamlet, or the naturalness of Coriolanus. Kean in
Shylock was natural; Bouffé in Père Grandet. Rachel
in Phèdre was natural; Farren in Grandfather Whitehead. Keeley in Waddilove was natural; Charles
Mathews in Affable Hawk, and Got in Maître Guérin.
Naturalness being truthfulness, it is obvious that a
coat-and-waistcoat realism demands a manner, delivery, and gesture wholly unlike the poetic realism
of tragedy and comedy; and it has been the great
mistake of actors that they have too often brought
with them into the drama of ordinary life the style
they have been accustomed to in the drama of ideal
life.

The modern French actors have seen the error;
and some English actors have followed their example, and aimed at greater quietness and "naturalness." At the Olympic this is attended with some
success. But even French actors, when not excellent, carry the reaction too far; and in the attempt
to be natural forget the *optique du théâtre*, and the
demands of art. They will sit upon side sofas, and
speak with their faces turned away from the audience, so that half their words are lost; and they will
lounge upon tables, and generally comport themselves in a manner which is not only easy, but free
and easy. The art of acting is not shown in giving a
conversational tone and a drawing-room quietness,
but in vividly presenting character, while never vio-
lating the proportions demanded on the one hand by

the *optique du théâtre*, and on the other by what the audience will recognize as truth.

This judgment, and the principles on which it was based, appear to have found little favor in certain quarters; and a writer in the *Reader* has attacked me in two columns of sarcasm and argument. He says, in reference to my article, that " few things are more painful than the nonsense which an exceedingly clever man may write about an art with which he has no real sympathy, to which he has ceased to give any serious thought." I leave it to my readers to appreciate my imperfect sympathy and want of serious thought ; as to the nonsense I may have written, everyone knows how easily a man may set down nonsense, and believe it to be sense. The point which most pressingly forces itself upon me is, that a writer who has given such prolonged and serious thought to the art of acting as my critic may be supposed to have given, should nevertheless have not yet mastered the initial principles on which that art rests. It is to me amazing how any man, writing *ex professo*, could cite Kean and Emil Devrient among natural actors, belonging to a " school of acting in which nature is carefully and closely followed, and in which small attention is paid to idealized impressions." I cannot explain how this writer's " serious thought " should have left him still in the condition of innocence which supposes that art is delusion, not illusion ; and that the nearer the approach to every-day vulgarity of detail the more consummate is the artistic effect.

In trying to disengage the question of " naturalness " from its ambiguities, I referred to the criticism

of Garrick's Hamlet which Fielding conveys through
the verdict of Partridge, my object being to discriminate between the nature of Hamlet and the
nature of Partridge ; and I said that if Fielding were
to be understood as correctly indicating Garrick's
manner, that manner must have been false to nature
and therefore bad art. On this my critic observes :
" The reasons for this remarkable opinion are very
shortly given. The melancholy, sceptical prince in
the presence of his father's ghost must have felt a
tremulous and solemn awe, but cannot have felt the
vulgar terror of a vulgar nature. The manner of a
frightened Partridge can never have been at all like
the manner of Hamlet. It is obvious that the naturalness required from Hamlet is very different from
the naturalness of a Partridge ; and Fielding made a
great mistake in assimilating the representation of
Garrick to the nature of a serving-man. Ordinary
people might find some difficulty in attaining the cer-
tainty which ' L.' has on his subject. Very few men
are so fortunate as to know a prince ; fewer still have
had the advantage of meeting ghosts ; it is therefore
difficult for most of us to realize so definitely as
' L.' does what the manner of a prince towards a
ghost would be. But the rather positive critic may
be assumed to be right. Probably, if a ghost walked
into Marlborough House, the manner of the Prince
of Wales towards the intruder would be very different
from that of the footman."

The answer to this is very simple. The manner of
Hamlet must be the manner consistent with that of
an ideal prince, and not the manner of a serving-man,

nor of one real prince, in Marlborough House or elsewhere. Had Shakspeare conceived a prince stupid,
feeble, weak-eyed, weak-chested, or bold, coarse, and
sensual, the actor would have been called upon to
represent the ideals of these. But having conceived
a *princely* Hamlet, *i. e.*, an accomplished, thoughtful,
dreamy young man—to represent him as frightened
at the ghost and behaving as a serving-man would
behave, was not natural, consequently not ideal, for
ideal treatment means treatment which is *true to the
nature of the character represented under the technical
conditions of the representation.*

This leads me to the main point at issue. I have
always emphatically insisted on the necessity of
actors being true to nature in the expression of natural emotions, although the technical conditions of
the art forbid the expressions being exactly those
of real life; but my critic, not understanding this,
says :

"In justice to 'L.,' however, it should be stated
that he does not altogether object to natural acting,
but only to acting which follows nature very closely.
Being a writer who constructs as well as destroys, he
explains what real dramatic art is. An actor should
impress an idealized image on the spectator's mind;
he should 'use natural expressions, but he must sublimate them,' whatever that may mean; his utterance
must be 'measured, musical, and incisive; his manner
typical and pictorial.'"

It is clear not only from this passage, but from the
examples afterwards cited, that my critic considers
the perfection of art to lie in the closest reproduction

of every-day experience. That an actor should raise
the natural expressions into ideal expressions—that
he should "sublimate" them—is so little understood
by my critic, that he professes not to know what sub-
limating "may mean." I will not insult him by supposing that it is the word which puzzles him, or that
he does not understand Dryden's verses:

> As his actions rose, so raise they still their vein,
> In words whose weight best suits a sublimated strain.

But I will ask him if he supposes that an actor, having to represent a character in situations altogether
exceptional, and speaking a language very widely departing from the language of ordinary life, would be
true to the nature of that character and that language,
by servilely reproducing the manners, expression, and
intonations of ordinary life? The poet is not closely
following nature; the poet is ideal in his treatment;
is the actor to be less so? I am presumed to have
been guilty of talking nonsense in requiring that the
musical verse of the poet should be spoken musically,
or the elaborate prose of the prose dramatist should
be spoken with measured cadence and incisive effect.
I cannot be supposed to approve of measured "mouthing," or to wish for turgidity in wishing for music
and precision; would the critic have verse declaimed
like prose (naturally, as it is falsely called), and prose
gabbled with little reference to cadence and emphasis,
like ordinary talk? When he objects to the manner
being typical, would he have it not to be recogniza-
ble? When he objects to the manner being pictorial,
would he have it careless, ungraceful, the slouching

of club-rooms and London streets carried into Verona or the Ardennes? Obviously, the pictorial manner which would be natural (ideal) to Romeo or Rosalind, would be unnatural in Charles Surface or Lady Teazle.

But so little does this writer discriminate between music and mouthing that he says:

"The performers may not come up to his standard, but it is satisfactory to think that their aim is in the right direction. No one will ever accuse Mr. Phelps or Mr. Creswick, or Miss Helen Faucit, of being too natural. These artists certainly have a highly ideal-ized style. Their utterance may not be musical, but it is measured and incisive—with a vengeance. On the French stage things are less satisfactory. Many of the leading actors there have a foolish hankering after nature. The silly people who think that French acting is sometimes admirable, and that English act-ing is generally execrable, should correct their opin-ions by studying the canons of a higher criticism; for the Paris actors have essentially shallow views of their art. Got, in that marvellous passage in 'Le Duc Job,' which has made grey-haired men cry like children, is much in error. He merely behaves just as a warm-hearted man would behave on suddenly re-ceiving the news of a dear friend's death; and this has been thought to make his performance so in-tensely touching. But it is quite wrong; his lan-guage is not 'measured, musical, and incisive,' his manner decidedly not 'typical and pictorial.' Sanson, with his satirical *bonhomie* in 'Le Fils de Giboyer,' has been much admired, because, having to act the Marquis d'Auberive, he was so precisely like a French nobleman of the old *régime*. His business, he should have learnt, was not to resemble a real marquis, but to 'impress the idealized image' of a marquis upon the spectator's mind. The terrible reality of Delaunay's acting in the last scene of 'On ne badine pas avec l'Amour' has made many spectators shudder; but then it is so perfectly natural, the expressions are not the least 'sublimated.' "

If he knew more of the French stage, he would, I think, have paused before writing such a passage. He would know that Rachel was supreme in virtue of those very qualities which he asserts the French actors to have relinquished in their hankering after nature; he would know that Mdme. Plessy is the most musical, the most measured, the most incisive speaker (whether of verse or prose) now on the stage; he would know that Got, Sanson, and Regnier are great actors, because they represent types, and the types are recognized as true.

When we are told that Got "merely behaves just as a warm-hearted man would behave on suddenly receiving the news of a dear friend's death," we ask *what* warm-hearted man? A hundred different men would behave in a hundred different ways on such an occasion, would say different things, would express their emotions with different looks and gestures. The actor has to select. He must be typical. His expressions must be those which, while they belong to the recognized symbols of our common nature, have also the peculiar individual impress of the character represented. It is obvious, to anyone who reflects for a moment, that nature is often so reticent

—that men and women express so little in their faces and gestures, or in their tones, of what is tearing their hearts—that a perfect copy of almost any man's expressions would be utterly ineffective on the stage. It is the actor's art to express in well-known symbols what an individual man may be supposed to feel, and we, the spectators, recognizing these expressions, are thrown into a state of sympathy. Unless the actor follows nature sufficiently to select symbols that are recognized as natural, he fails to touch us; but as to any minute fidelity in copying the actual manner of murderers, misers, avengers, broken-hearted fathers, etc., we really have had so little experience of such characters, that we cannot estimate the fidelity; hence the actor is forced to be as typical as the poet is. Neither pretends closely to copy nature, but only to represent nature sublimated into the ideal. The nearer the approach to every-day reality implied by the author in his characters and language—the closer the coat-and-waistcoat realism of the drama—the closer must be the actor's imitation of every-day manner; but even then he must idealize, *i. e.*, select and heighten—and it is for his tact to determine how much.

CHAPTER XI.

FOREIGN ACTORS ON OUR STAGE.

THAT our drama is extinct as literature, and our stage is in a deplorable condition of decline, no one ventures to dispute; but there are two opinions as to whether a revival is possible, or even probable; and various opinions as to the avenues through which such a revival may be approached. There are three obvious facts which may be urged against the suggestions of hope: these are, the gradual cessation of all attempts at serious dramatic literature, and their replacement by translations from the French, or adaptations from novels; the slow extinction of provincial theatres, which formed a school for the rearing of actors; and, finally, the accident of genius on our stage being unhappily rarer than ever. In the face of these undeniable facts, the hopeful are entitled to advance facts of equal importance on their side. Never in the history of our stage were such magnificent rewards within the easy grasp of talent; never were there such multitudes to welcome good acting. Only let the dramatist, or the actor, appear, and not London alone but all England, not England alone but all Europe, will soon resound with his name.

Dramatic literature may be extinct, but the dramatic instinct is ineradicable. The stage may be in a deplorable condition at present, but the delight in mimic representation is primal and indestructible. Thus it is that, in spite of people on all sides declaring that "they have ceased to go to the theatre," no sooner does an actor arise who is at all above the line, no sooner does a piece appear that has any special source of attraction, than the public flock to the theatre as it never flocked in what are called "the palmy days" of the drama. Fechter could play Hamlet for seventy consecutive nights: which to Garrick, Kemble, or Edmund Kean, would have sounded like the wildest hyperbole; and the greatest success of Liston and Mathews seems insignificant beside the success of Lord Dundreary. There is a ready answer to such facts conveyed in the sneer at public taste, and the assertion that all intelligence has departed, leaving only a vulgar craving for "sensation pieces." It is a cheap sneer. Sensation pieces are in the ascendant, but this is not because intelligence has departed, and there is no audience for better things, but simply because the number of pleasure-seekers is so much increased; and at all times the bulk of the public has cared less for art than amusement.* If intelligent people now go to witness inferior pieces, it is because better things are not produced: and sensation pieces, although appealing to the lowest faculties, do appeal to them effect-

* Et pour les sots acteurs
Dieu créa le faux goût et les sots spectateurs.
SANSON: *L'Art Théâtral.*

ively. If there are crowds to see the "Colleen
Bawn" and the "Duke's Motto," it is because these
pieces are really good of their kind; the kind may be
a low kind; but will anyone say that the legitimate
drama has of late years been represented in a style
to satisfy an intellectual audience? Who would
leave the "comforts of the Saut-market" for the
manifold discomforts of a theatre, unless some strong
intellectual or emotional stimulus were to be given in
exchange? and who can be expected to submit with
patience to lugubrious comedy and impossible tragedy,
such as has been offered of late years to the British
public? Considering that these "higher efforts" had
so dreary an effect, what wonder that even the intelligent public sought amusement in efforts which were
not so exalted, but really did amuse? A public seeks
amusement at the theatre, and turns impatiently from
dreariness to Dundreariness. Let an Edmund Kean
—or any faint approach to an Edmund Kean—appear
to-morrow, and the public will rush to see him as they
rushed to hear Jenny Lind: the mob, because easily
pleased, will rush to see anyone about whom the
world is talking; the intelligent public, because
always ready to welcome genius. The proof of this
eagerness to welcome any exceptional talent is seen
in the success of Fechter and Ristori; and, in another
direction, the proof of the deplorable condition of
our stage is seen in the success of Mdlle. Stella Colas.
Fechter and Ristori are both accomplished actors; not
great actors, but still, within the limits of their powers,
possessed of the mechanism of their art; gifted,
moreover, with physical and intellectual advantages

which render them admirable representatives of certain parts. Mdlle. Colas, on the contrary, though she is sweetly pretty, and has a sympathetic voice, and a great deal of untrained energy, is not yet an actress; there are only the possibilities of an actress in her.

The disadvantages of a language unfamiliar as a spoken language to the great bulk of the audience, and of companions who are scarcely on a level with the actors in the open-air theatres of Italy, have not prevented Ristori from achieving an immense success; nor have the terrible disadvantages of an intonation and pronunciation which play havoc with Shakspeare's lines prevented Fechter from "drawing the town." There is something of fashion in all this, of course; something to be attributed to the mere piquancy of the fact that Shakspeare is played by a French actor: but we must not exaggerate this influence. It may draw you to the theatre out of curiosity, but it will not stir your emotion when in the theatre; it will not bring down tumultuous applause at the great scenes. No sooner are you *moved*, than you forget the foreigner in the emotion. And the proof that it really is what is excellent, and not what is adventitious, which creates the triumph of Fechter in Hamlet, is seen in the supreme ineffectiveness of his Othello. In "Ruy Blas" and the "Corsican Brothers" he was recognized as an excellent actor—not by any means a great actor, very far from that; but one who in the present condition of the stage was considered a decided acquisition. He then played Hamlet, and gave a new and charming representation to a part in which no actor has been known to fail; hence the uncritical concluded that he was a great actor. But when he came to a part like Othello, which calls upon the rarest capabilities of an actor, the public then *remembered* that he was a foreigner, and discovered that he was not a tragedian.

His Hamlet was one of the very best, and his Othello one of the very worst, I have ever seen. On leaving the theatre after "Hamlet," I felt once more what a great play it was, with all its faults, and they are gross and numerous. On leaving the theatre after "Othello," I felt as if my old admiration for this supreme masterpiece of the art had been an exaggeration: all the faults of the play stood out so glaringly, all its beauties were so dimmed and distorted by the acting of every one concerned. It was necessary to recur to Shakspeare's pages to recover the old feeling.

Reflecting on the contrast offered by these two performances, it seemed to me that a good lesson on the philosophy of acting was to be read there. Two cardinal points were illustrated by it. First, the very general confusion which exists in men's minds respecting naturalism and idealism in art (which has been discussed in the last chapter); secondly, the essential limitation of an actor's sphere, as determined by his personality. Both in "Hamlet" and "Othello" Fechter attempts to be *natural*, and keeps as far away as possible from the conventional declamatory style, which is by many mistaken for idealism only because it is unlike reality. His physique enabled him to represent Hamlet, and his naturalism was artistic.

His physique wholly incapacitated him from representing Othello; and his naturalism, being mainly
determined by his personality, became utter feebleness. I do not mean that the whole cause of his
failure rests with his physical incapacity, for, as will
presently be shown, his conception of the part is as
questionable as his execution is feeble; but he might
have had a wrong conception of the part, and yet
have been ten times more effective, had nature endowed him with a physique of more weight and intensity. Twenty Othellos I have seen, with far less
intelligence, but with more effective representative
qualities, whose performances have stirred the very
depths of the soul; whereas I cannot imagine any
amount of intelligence enabling Fechter's personality
to make the performance satisfactory.

His Hamlet was " natural ;" but this was not owing
to the simple fact of its being more conversational
and less stilted than usual. If Shakspeare's grandest
language seemed to issue naturally from Fechter's
lips, and did not strike you as out of place, which it
so often does when mouthed on the stage, the reason
was that he formed a tolerably true conception of
Hamlet's nature, and could *represent* that conception.
It was his personality which enabled him to represent
this conception. Many of the spectators had a conception as true, or truer, but they could not have *represented* it. This is self-evident. Naturalism truly
means the reproduction of those details which *char-
acterize the nature of the thing represented.* Realism
means *truth*, not vulgarity: truth of the higher as

of the lower forms; truth of passion, and truth of manners. As Sanson finely says:

L'art c'est le naturel en doctrine érigé.

The nature of a Macbeth is not the nature of an Othello; the speech of Achilles is not the speech of Thersites. The truth of the " Madonna di San Sisto" is not the truth of Murillo's " Beggar Girl." But artists and critics often overlook this. Actors are especially prone to overlook it, and, in trying to be *natural*, they sink into the *familiar;* though that is as unnatural as if they were to attempt to heighten the reality of the Apollo by flinging a paletot over his naked shoulders. It is this error into which Fechter falls in Othello; he vulgarizes the part in the attempt to make it natural. Instead of the heroic, grave, impassioned Moor, he represents an excitable creole of our own day.

Intellectually and physically his Hamlet so satis- fies the audience that they exclaim, " How natural!" Hamlet is fat, according to his mother's testimony; but he is also—at least in Ophelia's eyes—very handsome—

> The courtier's, soldier's, scholar's eye, tongue, sword,
> The glass of fashion and the mould of form,
> The observed of all observers.

Fechter is lymphatic, delicate, handsome, and with his long flaxen curls, quivering, sensitive nostrils, fine eye, and sympathetic voice, perfectly represents the graceful prince. His aspect and bearing are such that the eye rests on him with delight. Our sympathies are

completely secured. All those scenes which demand
the qualities of an accomplished comedian he plays
to perfection. Seldom have the scenes with the players, with Polonius, with Horatio, with Rosenkranz
and Guildenstern, or the quieter monologues, been
better played; they are touched with so cunning a
grace, and a manner so *natural*, that the effect is delightful. We not only feel in the presence of an individual, a character, but feel that the individual is
consonant with our previous conception of Hamlet,
and with the part assigned him in the play. The passages of *emotion* also are rendered with some sensibility. His delightful and sympathetic voice, and the
unforced fervor of his expression, triumph over the foreigner's accent and the foreigner's mistakes in emphasis.
This is really a considerable triumph; for although
Fechter pronounces English very well for a Frenchman, it is certain that his accent greatly interferes
with the due effect of the speeches. But the foreign
accent is as nothing compared with the frequent error
of emphasis; and *this* surely he might overcome by
diligent study, if he would consent to submit to the
rigorous criticism of some English friend, who would
correct him every time he errs. The sense is often
perturbed, and sometimes violated, by this fault. Yet
so great is the power of true emotion that even *this*
is forgotten directly he touches the feelings of the
audience; and in his great speech, "O what a rogue
and peasant slave am I!" no one hears the foreigner.

Physically then we may say that his Hamlet is
perfectly satisfactory; nor is it intellectually open
to more criticism than must always arise in the case

of a character which admits of so many readings. It is certainly a fine conception, consonant in general with what the text of Shakspeare indicates. It is the nearest approach I have seen to the realization of Goethe's idea, expounded in the celebrated critique in *Wilhelm Meister*, that there is a burden laid on Hamlet too heavy for his soul to bear. The refinement, the feminine delicacy, the vacillation of Hamlet are admirably represented : and it is only in the more tragic scenes that we feel any shortcoming. For these scenes he wants the tragedian's *personality;* and once for all let me say that by *personality* I do not simply mean the qualities of voice and person, but the qualities which give the force of animal passion demanded by tragedy, and which cannot be *represented* except by a certain animal power.

There is one point, however, in his reading of the part which seems to me manifestly incorrect. The error, if error it be, is not peculiar to him, but has been shared by all the other Hamlets, probably because they did not know how to represent what Shakspeare has *indicated* rather than expressly set down. And as there is nothing in his physique which would prevent the proper representation of a different conception, I must assume that the error is one of interpretation.

Much discussion has turned on the question of Hamlet's madness, whether it be real or assumed. It is not possible to settle this question. Arguments are strong on both sides. He may be really mad, and yet, with that terrible consciousness of the fact which often visits the insane, he may " put an antic disposition on," as a sort of relief to his feelings. Or he may merely assume madness as a means of accounting for any extravagance of demeanor into which the knowledge of his father's murder may betray him. Shakspeare has committed the serious fault of not making this point clear; a modern writer who should commit such a fault would get no pardon. The actor is by no means called upon to settle such points. One thing, however, he is called upon to do, and that is, not to depart widely from the text, not to misrepresent what stands plainly written. Yet this the actors do in Hamlet. They may believe that Shakspeare never meant Hamlet to be really mad; but they cannot deny, and should not disregard, the plain language of the text—namely, that Shakspeare meant Hamlet to be in a state of *intense cerebral excitement*, seeming like madness. His sorrowing nature has been suddenly ploughed to its depths by a horror so great as to make him recoil every moment from the belief in its reality. The shock, if it has not destroyed his sanity, has certainly *unsettled* him. Nothing can be plainer than this. Every line speaks it. We see it in the rambling incoherence of his "wild and whirling words" to his fellow-watchers and fellow-witnesses; but as *this* may be said to be assumed by him (although the motive for such an assumption is not clear, as he might have "put them off," and yet retained his coherence), I will appeal to the impressive fact of the irreverence with which in this scene he speaks *of* his father and *to* his father— language which Shakspeare surely never meant to be

insignificant, and which the actors always *omit*. Here
is the scene after the exit of the ghost :

Enter HORATIO *and* MARCELLUS.

Mar. How is't, my noble lord ?

Hor. What news, my lord ?

Ham. O, wonderful !

Hor. Good, my lord, tell it.

Ham. No ;
You'll reveal it.

Hor. Not I, my lord, by heaven.

Mar. Nor I, my lord.

Ham. How say you then ; would heart of man once think it ?
But you'll be secret—

Hor., Mar. Ay, by heaven, my lord.

Ham. There's ne'er a villain, dwelling in all Denmark—
But he's an arrant knave.

Hor. There needs no ghost , my lord, come from the grave,
To tell us this.

Ham. Why, right ; you are in the right ;
And so, without more circumstance at all,
I hold it fit that we shake hands, and part ;
You, as your business and desire shall point you—
For every man has business and desire,
Such as it is—and for mine own poor part,
Look you, I'll go pray.

Hor. These are but wild and whirling words, my lord.

Ham. I'm sorry they offend you, heartily :
Yes, 'faith, heartily.

Hor. There's no offence, my lord.

Ham. Yes, by St. Patrick, but there is, my lord.
And much offence too, touching this vision here.
It is an honest ghost, *that* let me tell you ;
For your desire to know what is between us,
O'ermaster it as you may. And now, good friends,
As you are friends, scholars and soldiers,
Give me one poor request.

Hor. What is't, my lord ?
We will.

Ham. Never make known what you have seen to-night
Hor., Mar. My lord, we will not.
Ham.   Nay, but swear't.
Hor.   In faith,
My lord, not I.
Mar.   Nor I, my lord, in faith.
Ham. Upon my sword.
Mar.   We have sworn, my lord, already.
Ham. Indeed, upon my sword, indeed.
Ghost. [*Beneath.*] Swear.
Ham. Ha, ha, boy! say'st thou so? art thou there, truepenny?
Come on—*you hear this fellow in the cellerage*—
Consent to swear.
    Hor.   Propose the oath, my lord.
    Ham. Never to speak of this that you have seen.
Swear by my sword.
    Ghost. [*Beneath.*] Swear.
    Ham. Hic et ubique? then we'll shift our ground :—
Come hither, gentlemen,
And lay your hands again upon my sword :
Never to speak of this that you have heard,
Swear by my sword.
    Ghost. [*Beneath.*] Swear.
    *Ham. Well said, old mole! canst work i' the ground so fast?
A worthy pioneer!*—Once more remove, good friends.

Now, why are these irreverent words omitted?
Because the actors feel them to be irreverent, incongruous? If spoken as Shakspeare meant them
to be—as Hamlet in his excited and bewildered state
must have uttered them—they would be eminently
significant. It is evading the difficulty to omit them;
and it is a departure from Shakspeare's obvious intention. Let but the actor enter into the excitement of
the situation, and make *visible* the hurrying agitation
which prompts these wild and whirling words, he

will then find them expressive, and will throw the audience into corresponding emotion.

But this scene is only the beginning. From the moment of the Ghost's departure Hamlet is a *changed* man. All the subsequent scenes should be impregnated with vague horror, and an agitation compounded of feverish desire for vengeance with the perplexities of thwarting doubt as to the reality of the story which has been heard. This alternation of wrath, and of doubt as to whether he has not been the victim of an hallucination, should be represented by the feverish agitation of an unquiet mind, visible even under all the outward calmness which it may be necessary to put on; whereas the Hamlets I have seen are perfectly calm and self-possessed when they are not in a tempest of rage, or not feigning madness to deceive the king.

It is part and parcel of this erroneous conception as to the state of Hamlet's mind (unless it be the mistake of substituting declamation for acting) which, as I believe, entirely misrepresents the purport of the famous soliloquy—"To be, or not to be." This is not a set speech to be declaimed to pit, boxes, and gallery, nor is it a moral thesis debated by Hamlet in intellectual freedom; yet one or the other of these two mistakes is committed by all actors. Because it is a fine speech, pregnant with thought, it has been mistaken for an oratorical display; but I think Shakspeare's genius was too eminently dramatic to have committed so great an error as to substitue an oration for an exhibition of Hamlet's state of mind. The speech is passionate, not reflective; and it should be so spoken as if the thoughts were *wrung* from the agonies of a soul hankering after suicide as an escape from evils, yet terrified at the dim sense of greater evils after death. Not only would such a reading of the speech give it tenfold dramatic force, but it would be the fitting introduction to the wildness of the scene, which immediately succeeds, with Ophelia. This scene has also been much discussed. To render its strange violence intelligible, actors are wont to indicate, by their looking towards the door, that they suspect the king, or some one else, to be watching; and the wildness then takes its place among the *assumed* extravagances of Hamlet. Fechter also conceives it thus. I cannot find any warrant in Shakspeare for such a reading; and it is adopted solely to evade a difficulty which no longer exists when we consider Hamlet's state of feverish excitement. I believe, therefore, that Hamlet is not disguising his real feelings in this scene, but is terribly in earnest. If his wildness seem unnatural, I would ask the actors what they make of the far *greater* extravagance with which he receives the confirmation of his doubts by the effect of the play upon the king? Here, it is to be observed, there is no pretext for assuming an extravagant demeanor; no one is watching now; he is alone with his dear friend and confidant, Horatio; and yet note his conduct. Seeing the king's guilt, he exclaims:

His name's Gonzago ; the story is extant, and writ in choice Italian ; you shall see anon, how the murtherer gets the love of Gonzago's wife.
Oph. The king rises.
Ham. What ! frighted with false fire !

Queen. How fares my lord ?
Pol. Give o'er the play.
King. Give me some light :—away !
All. Lights, lights, lights !

[*Exeunt all but* HAM. *and* HOR.

Ham. Why, let the strucken deer go weep,
   The hart ungalled play :
For some must watch, while some must sleep ;
   So runs the world away.—
Would not this, sir, and a forest of feathers (if the rest of my fortunes turn Turk with me), with two Provençal roses on my razed shoes, get me a fellowship in a cry of players, sir ?
   Hor. Half a share.
   Ham. A whole one, ay.
For thou dost know, O Damon dear,
   This realm dismantled was
Of Jove himself ; and now reigns here
   A very, very peacock.
   Hor. You might have rhymed.
   Ham. O good Horatio, I'll take the ghost's word for a thousand pound. Didst perceive ?
   Hor. Very well, my lord.
   Ham. Upon the talk of the poisoning—
   Hor. I did very well note him.
   Ham. Ha, ha !—Come, some music ; come, the recorders.—
For if the king like not the comedy,
Why, then, belike, he likes it not, perdy.

Of course the actors omit the most significant of these passages, because they are afraid of being comic; but, if given with the requisite wildness, these passages would be terrible in their grotesqueness. It is true that such wildness and grotesqueness would be out of keeping with any representation of Hamlet which made him calm, and only assuming madness at intervals. But is such a conception Shakspearian?

Fechter is not specially to be blamed for not hav-

ing made Hamlet's state of excitement visible
throughout; but although his personality debars him
from due representation of the more tragic scenes, it
would not debar him from representing Hamlet's
agitation if he conceived it truly. On the whole,
however, I repeat that his performance was charming, because natural.

In direct contrast was the performance of Othello.
It had no one good quality. False in conception, it
was feeble in execution. He attempted to make the
character natural, and made it vulgar. His idea of
the character and of the play from first to last
showed strange misconception. He departed openly
from the plain language of the text, on points where
there is no justification for the departure. Thus,
Othello tells us he is "declined into the vale of
years;" Fechter makes him young. Othello is black
—the very tragedy lies there; the whole force of the
contrast, the whole pathos and extenuation of his
doubts of Desdemona, depend on this blackness.
Fechter makes him a half-caste, whose mere appearance would excite no repulsion in any woman out of
America. Othello is grave, dignified, a man accustomed to the weight of great reponsibilities, and to
the command of armies; Fechter is unpleasantly
familiar, paws Iago about like an overdemonstrative
school-boy; shakes hands on the slightest provocation; and bears himself like the hero of French
drame, but not like a hero of tragedy.

In his edition of the play Fechter urges two considerations. First, that Shakspeare is to be acted,
not recited; secondly, that *tradition* ought to be set

aside. In both points he will find most people agree-
ing with him, but few willing to see any novelty in
these positions. We, who remember Kean in Othello,
may surely be excused if we believe that we have
seen Othello *acted*, and so acted as there is little
chance of our seeing it acted again; the consequence
of which is, that we look upon Fechter's representation as acting, indeed, but as very bad acting.

Then as to tradition, we are willing enough, now-
adays, to give up all conventional business which
does not justify itself; but we are very far from supposing that, because Fechter's arrangement of the
business is new, therefore it is justifiable or acceptable. In some respects it is good; in the arrangement of the scene in the senate there was a very
striking improvement, which gave a really natural air
to the scene; and some other scenical details show a
decided faculty for stage arrangement. But in many
others there is a blundering perversity and disregard
of the obvious meaning of the text, which is only to
be accounted for on the supposition that Fechter
wished to make "Othello" a *drame* such as would suit
the Porte St. Martin.

The principle has doubtless been the same as that
which, in a less degree, and under happier inspiration,
made the success of "Hamlet": the desire to be natural—the aim at realism. But here the confusion between realism and vulgarism works like poison. It
is not consistent with the nature of tragedy to ob-
trude the details of daily life. All that lounging on
tables and lolling against chairs, which help to convey
a sense of reality in the *drame*, are as unnatural in

tragedy as it would be to place the "Sleeping Fawn" of Phidias on a comfortable feather-bed. When Fechter takes out his door-key to let himself into his house, and, on coming back, relocks the door and pockets the key, the *intention* is doubtless to give an air of reality; the *effect* is to make us forget the "noble Moor," and to think of a sepoy. When he appears leaning on the shoulder of Iago (the great general and his ensign!), when he salutes the personages with graceful prettinesses, when he kisses the hand of Desdemona, and when he employs that favorite gesticulation which reminds us but too forcibly of a *gamin* threatening to throw a stone, he is certainly *natural*—but according to whose nature?

In general, it may be said that, accomplished an actor as Fechter certainly is, he has allowed the acting manager to gain the upper hand. In his desire to be effective by means of small details of "business," he has entirely frittered away the great effects of the drama. He has yet to learn the virtue of simplicity; he has yet to learn that tragedy acts through the emotions, and not through the eye; whatever distracts attention from the passion of the scene is fatal.

Thus, while his Hamlet satisfied the audience by being at once naturally conceived and effectively represented, his Othello left the audience perfectly cold, or interested only as by a curiosity, because it was unnaturally conceived and feebly executed. Had the execution been fine, the false conception would have been forgotten or pardoned. Many a ranting Othello contrives to interest and to move his audience without any conception at all, simply uttering the language of

Shakspeare with force, and following the traditional business. Shakspeare, if the personality of the actor be not too violently in contradiction with the text, carries effect in every scene; we listen and are moved. But unhappily Fechter's personality is one wholly unsuited to such a character as Othello. This is evident from the first. My doubts began with the first act. In it Othello has little *to do*, but much *to be*. In this masterpiece of dramatic exposition the groundwork of the play is grandly laid out. It presents the hero as a great and trusted warrior, a simple, calm, open, reliant nature—a man admirable not only in his deeds, but in his lofty and heroic soul. Unless you get a sense of this, you are as puzzled at Desdemona's choice as Brabantio is. But it is inevitable that with such a personality as Fechter's you should feel none of this. He represents an affectionate but feeble young gentleman, whose position in the army must surely have been gained by "purchase." This is not the actor's fault. Even had he been calm and simple in his gestures, he could not have been dignified and impressive; nature had emphatically said No to such an effect. Voice and bearing would have failed him had his conception been just. An unintelligent actor, who is at the same time a superb animal, will be impressive in this act if he is simply quiet. If, for example, you compare Gustavus Brooke with Fechter, you will see this at once. Still more strikingly is this seen on a comparison of Edmund Kean with Fechter. Kean was undersized—very much smaller than Fechter; and yet what a grand bearing he had! what an impressive personality!

In the second act my doubts increased. The entrance of Othello, with the flame of victory in his eye, eager to clasp his young wife to his breast, and share with her his triumph and his joy, was an opportunity for being *natural* which Fechter wholly missed. Never was there a tamer meeting. Kean's tones, "O my fair warrior!" are still ringing in my ears, though a quarter of a century must have elapsed since I heard them; but I cannot recall Fechter's tones, heard only the other night. I only recall a vision of him holding his wife at most "proper" distance, kissing her hand, his tone free from all tremulous emotion, though he has to say:

O my soul's joy!
If after every tempest come such calms,
May the winds blow till they have wakened death!
If it were now to die
'Twere now to be most happy; for I fear
My soul hath her content so absolute,
That not another comfort like to this
Succeeds in unknown fate.

And from Desdemona he turns to the gentlemen of Cyprus, as affable and calm as if he had but just come home from a morning stroll. There was none of the emotion of the situation. ·

In the scene of the brawl we have the first indication of Othello's tremendous vehemence when roused. Fechter was loud, but he was not fierce.* It is char-

* Fuyant le naturel sans trouver la grandeur.
Sanson: *L'Art Théâtral*

acteristic of his whole performance in the passionate parts, that he goes up the stage and bids them

> Silence that *dreadful* bell, it frights the isle
> From her propriety,

with an accent of impatient irritability, as if he were angry at the bell's preventing his hearing what was to be said.

But little as the performance in these two acts came up to even my moderate expectations of Fechter's power to represent Othello, it was not until the third act that I finally pronounced judgment. That act is the test of a tragedian. If he cannot produce a great effect there, he need never seek elsewhere for an opportunity ; the greatest will find in it occasion for all his powers, and the worst will hardly miss some effects. To think of what Edmund Kean was in this act! When shall we see again that lion-like power and lion-like grace—that dreadful culmination of wrath, alternating with bursts of agony—that Oriental and yet most natural gesture, which even in its *naturalness* preserved a grand ideal propriety (for example, when his joined uplifted hands, the palms being upwards, were lowered upon his head, as if to keep his poor brain from bursting)—that exquisitely touching pathos, and that lurid flame of vengeance flashing from his eye? When shall we hear again those tones: " Not a jot, not a jot "—" Blood, Iago, blood "— " But oh, the pity of it, Iago! the pity of it "? Certainly no one ever expected that Fechter, with his sympathetic temperament and soft voice, could approach the tragic grandeur of the elder Kean: but neither could anyone who had heard that his Othello was "the talk of the town" have supposed that this third act would fail even to move the applause of an audience very ready to applaud.

In saying that he failed to arouse the audience I am saying simply what I observed and felt. The causes of that failure may be open to discussion: the fact is irresistible; and the causes seem to me clear enough. He is incapable of representing the torrent of passion, which by him is broken up into numerous petty waves: we see the glancing foam, breaking along many lines, instead of one omnipotent and roaring surf. He is loud—and weak; irritable, not passionate. The wrath escapes in spurts, instead of flowing in one mighty tide; and after each spurt he is calm, not shaken by the tremulous subsidence of passion. This lapse from the wildness of rage to the calmness of logical consideration or argumentative expostulation, this absence of gradation and *afterglow* of passion, I have already indicated as the error committed by Charles Kean and other tragedians; it arises from their not identifying themselves with the feeling of the part.

To give what Bacon calls an "ostensive instance," let me refer to the opening of the fourth act. Othello, worked upon by Iago's horrible suggestions, is so shaken by wrath and grief that he falls down in a fit. Fechter, probably because he felt that he could not render the passion so as to make this natural, omits the scene, and opens the act with Iago soliloquizing over his senseless victim. In spite of the awkward attitude in which Fechter is lying, those of the audience who are not familiar with the play imagine that Othello is *sleeping;* and when he rises from the couch and begins to speak, he is indeed as calm and unaffected by the fit as if he had only been asleep.

Another source of weakness is the redundancy of gesture and the desire to make a number of points, instead of concentrating attention on the general effect. Thus, when he is roused to catch Iago by the throat, instead of an accumulation of threats, he jerks out a succession of various threats, looking *away* from Iago every now and then, and varying his gestures, so as to destroy all sense of climax.

If it is a fact—and I appeal to the audience as witness—that we do not feel deep pity for the noble Moor, and do not sympathize with his irrational yet natural wrath, when Fechter plays the part, surely the reason can only be that the part is not represented *naturally*. Now much of this, I repeat, is the necessary consequence of his personality. He could not represent it naturally even if he conceived the part truly; and as already intimated, the conception is not true. Certain points of the conception have been touched on; I will now specify two others. The unideal (consequently unnatural) representation may be illustrated by the manner in which he *proposes*, instead of ordering, Cassio's death. Shakspeare's language is peremptory

> Within these three days let me hear thee say
> That Cassio's not alive.

The idea in his mind is simply that Cassio has deserved death. He does not trouble himself about the means; and surely never thinks of *murder*. A general who orders a soldier to be hung, or shot, without trial, is not a murderer. Yet Fechter *proposes* a murder, and proposes it with a sort of subdued hesitation, as if conscious of the crime. He thus completely bears out Rymer's sarcasm: "He sets Iago to the fighting part, to kill Cassio; and chuses himself to murder the silly woman, his wife, that was like to make no resistance."*

The second illustration which may be noticed is the perverse departure from the obvious meaning of the text, which, in his desire for originality and naturalness in the business, makes him destroy the whole art of Shakspeare's preparation, and makes the jealousy of Othello seem preposterous. One defect in the play which has been felt by all critics is the rapidity with which Othello is made to believe in his wife's guilt. Now, allowing for the rapidity which the compression necessary to dramatic art renders almost inevitable, I think Shakspeare has so exhibited the *growth* of the jealousy, that it is only on reflection that the audience becomes aware of the slight grounds on which the Moor is convinced. It is the actor's part to make the audience feel this growth —to make them go along with Othello, sympathizing with him, and *believing* with him. Fechter deliberately disregards all the plain meaning of the text,

* RYMER: *A Short View of Tragedy, its original excellency and corruption.* 1693. P. 93. This most amusing attack on Othello reads very often like sound criticism, when one has just witnessed the performances at the Princess' Theatre.

and makes the conviction sudden and preposterous. It is one of his new arrangements that Othello, when the tempter begins his diabolical insinuation, shall be seated at a table reading and signing papers. When first I heard of this bit of "business," it struck me as admirable; and indeed I think so still; although the manner in which Fechter executes it is one of those lamentable examples in which the *dramatic* art is subordinated to serve *theatrical* effect.* That Othello should be seated over his papers, and should reply to Iago's questions while continuing his examination, and affixing his signature, is *natural;* but it is not natural—that is, not true to the nature of Othello and the situation—for him to be dead to the dreadful import of Iago's artful suggestions. Let us hear Shakspeare.

Othello and Iago enter as Cassio takes leave of Desdemona; whereupon Iago says, meaning to be heard, "Ha! I like not that!"

Othello. What dost thou say?
Iago. Nothing, my lord: or if—I know not what.
Othello. Was not that Cassio parted from my wife?
Iago. Cassio, my lord? no, sure, I cannot think it,
That he would *steal away,* so *guilty-like,*
Seeing *your coming.*
Othello. I do believe 'twas he.
Desdem. How now, my lord.
I have been talking with a suitor here,
A man that languishes in your displeasure.
Othello. Who is't you mean?

* Having now seen Salvini in Othello I conclude that this "business" was imitated from him—but Fechter failed to imitate the expression of emotion which renders such business significant.

Des. Why, your lieutenant Cassio ; good my lord.
If I have any grace or power to move you,
His present reconciliation take.
I prithee call him back.
    Othello. Went he hence now?
    Des. Ay, sooth ; so humbled
That he hath left part of his grief with me
To suffer with him. Good love, call him back.
    Othello. Not now, sweet Desdemona ; some other time.
    Des. But shall't be shortly ?
    Othello. The sooner, sweet, for you.
    Des. Shall't be to-night at supper ?
    Othello. No, not to-night.
    Des. To-morrow, dinner, then ?
    Othello. I shall not dine at home.

These short evasive sentences are subtly expressive
of the state of Othello's mind; but Fechter misrepresents them by making Othello free from all misgiv-
ing.   He "toys with her curls," and treats her as a
father might treat a child who was asking some favor
which could not be granted, yet which called for no
explicit refusal.   If the scene stood alone, I should
read it differently; but standing as it does between
the two attempts of Iago to fill Othello's mind with
suspicion, the meaning is plain enough.   He has been
made uneasy by Iago's remarks; very naturally, his
bearing towards his wife reveals that uneasiness.   A
vague feeling, which he dares not shape into a suspicion, disturbs him.   She conquers him at last by her
winning ways; and he vows that he will deny her
nothing.

If this be the state of mind in which the great
scene begins, it is obviously a serious mistake in
Fechter to sit down to his papers, perfectly calm,

free from all idea whatever of what Iago has suggested, and answering Iago's insidious questions as if
he did not divine their import. So clearly does
Othello divine their import, that it is *he*, and not
Iago, who expresses in words their meaning. It is
one of the artifices of Iago to make his victim draw
every conclusion from premises which are put before
him, so that, in the event of detection, he can say, " I
said nothing, I made no accusation." All he does is
to lead the thoughts of Othello to the conclusion
desired. The scene thus begins:

Iago. My noble lord—
Othello. What dost thou say, Iago?
Iago. Did Michael Cassio, when you wooed my lady,
Know of your love?

Now Iago perfectly well knew this, for he had heard
Desdemona say so just the minute before.

Othello. He did from first to last. Why dost thou ask?
Iago. But for the satisfaction of my thought;
No further harm.

Properly, Iago's answer should end at the word
thought; that is the answer to the question; but he
artfully adds the suggestion of harm, which falls like
a spark on the inflammable mind of his victim, who
eagerly asks, "Why of thy thought, Iago?"

Iago. I did not think he had been acquainted with her.
Othello. Oh, yes; and went between us very oft.
Iago. Indeed?
Othello. Indeed? Ay, indeed. Discern'st thou aught in that?
Is he not honest?

Iago. Honest, my lord?
Othello. Honest? ay, honest?
Iago. My lord, for aught I know.
Othello. What dost thou think?
Iago. Think, my lord?

It is difficult to comprehend how anyone should fail to interpret this dialogue, every word of which is an increase of the slowly growing suspicion. If the scene ended here, there might indeed be a defence set up for Fechter's notion that Othello should reply to the insinuation in a careless manner, " playing with his pen as he speaks;" but no defence is permissible for one moment when we know how the scene proceeds.

Othello. Think, my lord?   By heaven, he echoes me !
As if there were *some monster* in his thought
Too hideous to be shown.   Thou *dost mean something;*
I heard thee say but now, thou lik'dst not that
When Cassio left my wife : what didst not like?
And when I told thee he was of my counsel
In my whole course of wooing, thou cry'dst, indeed?
And didst contract and purse thy brow together,
As if thou then hadst shut up in thy brain
Some horrible conceit.   If thou dost love me
Show me thy thought.

Fechter would perhaps urge that this language is not to be understood seriously, but as the banter of Othello at seeing Iago purse his brow and look mysterious about trifles.   It is in this sense that he plays the part.   But how widely he errs, and how seriously Othello is disturbed, may be read in his next speech :

I know thou'rt full of love and honesty,
And weigh'st thy words before thou giv'st them breath,

Therefore these stops of thine *fright me the more;*
For such things in a *false disloyal knave*
Are tricks of custom ; but in a man that's just
They're close denotements, working from the heart
That passion cannot rule.

Is this banter? and when he bids Iago

Speak to me, as to thy thinkings,
As thou dost ruminate ; and *give thy worst of thoughts*
The worst of words,

it is impossible to suppose that his mind has not
already shaped the worst suspicions which he wishes
Iago to confirm.

Here, I affirm, the plain sense of Shakspeare is not
only too clearly indicated to admit of the most ingenious reading in another sense, but any other reading
would destroy the dramatic art with which the scene
is conducted, because it would destroy those indications of the *growth* of the feeling, which feeling,
being really founded on Iago's suggestions and the
smallest possible external evidence, becomes preposterous when the evidence alone is appealed to. Now
Fechter so little understands this as not only to miss
such broadly marked indications, but to commit the
absurdity of making Othello *suddenly* convinced, and
by what? by the *argument* of Iago, that Desdemona
deceived her father, and may therefore deceive her
husband! But *that* argument (setting aside the
notion of a character like Othello being moved by

merely intellectual considerations) had already been
forcibly presented to his mind by her father:

> Look to her, Moor, have a quick eye to see:
> She did deceive her father, and may thee.

Whereupon he replies, "My life upon her faith."
And so he would reply to Iago, had not his mind
already been filled with distrust.   Fechter makes him
careless, confident, unsuspicious, until Iago suggests
her deception of her father, and then *at once* credu-
lous and overcome.   This may be the art of the
Porte St. Martin, or the Variétés; it is not the art
of Shakspeare.

Whatever may be our estimate of Fechter, his success with Hamlet proves that there is a vast and
hungry public ready to welcome and reward any good
dramatist or fine actor; but in default of these, willing
to be amused by *spectacles* and sensation pieces.
Whether dramatist or actor will arise, and by his
influence create a stage once more, is a wider question.   I shall not enter upon it here, nor shall I touch
on the causes of the present condition.   My purpose
is rather to consider the suggestion which has been
made of the probable influence of foreign actors upon
our stage.   Some have thought that here is an opportunity for our young actors to surprise many of the
secrets of the art, and to unlearn some of their own
conventional errors.   In one sense this is plausible;
for a young student, if at once gifted and modest,
may undeniably learn much in the study of artists
belonging to a wholly different school; especially if
he can discriminate what is conventional in them,

though unlike his own conventionalism. Nevertheless, on the whole, I think the gain likely to be small ;
just as the gain to our painters is small if they are
early sent to Rome to study the great masters. They
become imitators and imitate what is conventional,
or individual mannerism.

There is a mistake generally made respecting foreign actors, one, indeed, which is almost inevitable,
unless the critic has long been familiar with the foreign
stage. I allude to the mistake of supposing an actor
to be fresh and original because he has not the conventionalisms with which we are familiar on our own
stage. He has the conventionalisms of his own. The
traditions of the French, German, and Italian theatres
thus appear to our unfamiliar eyes as the inventions of
the actors; just as in our youth we thought it deliciously comic when the rattling young gentleman
placed his cane on the gouty old gentleman's toe—a
bit of "business" which now affects us with the
hilarity of an old Joe Miller. When Emil Devrient
played Hamlet with the German company, both he
and the actor who took the part of Polonius were
thought by our old play-goers to be remarkable artists,
simply because the "business" was so very novel.
But any one familiar with the German stage could
have assured them that this business was almost all
traditional, and could have pointed out the extremely
mechanical style in which the parts were performed
by these actors. It is true that English actors might
have gained some hints from studying these representations; but only by discriminating those elements

which fitly belong to the characters from those which were German conventionalisms.

Thus, I do not know that under any circumstances the presence of foreign actors on our stage could have more than the negative influence of teaching our actors to avoid some of their conventionalisms. It could only have a direct and positive influence in the case of real genius, which would display the futility of conventionalisms, and teach the actor to rely on sincerity of expression. When great effects are seen to be produced by the natural language of emotion, the intelligent actor loses his confidence in rant.

Passing from these general considerations to the special case of the foreign actors now on our stage, let us ask what probability is there of any good influence being derived from such models? Ristori is universally spoken of as the rival of Rachel: many think her superior. The difference between them seems to me the difference between talent and genius, between a woman admirable in her art, and a woman creative in her art. Ristori has complete mastery of the mechanism of the stage, but is without the inspiration necessary for great acting. A more beautiful and graceful woman, with a more musical voice, has seldom appeared; but it is with her acting as with her voice—the line which separates charm from profound emotion is never passed. When I saw her in Lady Macbeth my disappointment was extreme: none of the qualities of a great actress were manifested. But she completely conquered me in Medea; and the conquest was all the more noticeable because it triumphed over the impressions previously received from Robson's burlesque imitation. The exquisite grace of her attitudes, the mournful beauty of her voice, the flash of her wrath, and the air of supreme *distinction* which seems native to her, gave a charm to this performance which is unforgettable. No wonder that people were enthusiastic about an actress who could give them such refined pleasure; and no wonder that few paused to be very critical of her deficiencies. I missed, it is true, the *something* which Rachel had: the sudden splendor of creative power, the burning-point of passion; yet I confess that I then thought it possible she might prove a more consummate comedian than Rachel, though so manifestly inferior to her in great moments. That supposition was a profound mistake. I discovered it on seeing Adrienne Lecouvreur the other night. The disappointment, not to say weariness, felt at this performance, caused me to recur to the disappointment felt at her Lady Macbeth: these performances marked a limit, and defined the range of her artistic power. In Adrienne there was still the lovely woman, with the air of distinction and the musical voice; but except in the recitation of the pretty fable of the two pigeons, the passage from Phèdre, and the one look of dawning belief brightening into rapture, as she is reassured by her lover's explanation, there was nothing in the performance which was not thoroughly conventional. Nor was this the worst fault. In the lighter scenes she was not only conventional, but committed that common mistake of conventional actors, an incongruous *mixture* of effects. Let me explain more particularly what is meant by the term conventional acting. When an actor feels a vivid sympathy with the passion, or humor, he is representing, he *personates*, *i. e.*, speaks through the *persona* or character; and for the moment *is* what he *represents*. He can do this only in proportion to the vividness of his sympathy, and the plasticity of his organization, which enables him to give *expression* to what he feels; there are certain physical limitations in every organization which absolutely prevent adequate expression of what is in the mind; and thus it is that a dramatist can rarely personate one of his own conceptions. But within the limits which are assigned by nature to every artist, the success of the personation will depend upon the vividness of the actor's sympathy, and his honest reliance on the truth of his own individual expression, in preference to the conventional expressions which may be accepted on the stage. This is the great actor, the creative artist. The conventional artist is one who either, because he does not feel the vivid sympathy, or cannot express what he feels, or has not sufficient energy of self-reliance to trust frankly to his own expressions, cannot *be* the part, but tries to *act* it, and is thus necessarily driven to adopt those conventional means of expression with which the traditions of the stage abound. Instead of allowing a strong feeling to express itself through its natural signs, he seizes upon the conventional signs, either because in truth there is no strong feeling moving him, or because he is not artist enough to give it genuine expression; his lips will curl, his brow wrinkle, his eyes be thrown up, his forehead be slapped, or he will grimace, rant, and

" take the stage," in the style which has become traditional, but which was perhaps never seen off the
stage; and thus he runs through the gamut of sounds
and signs which bear as remote an affinity to any reai
expressions as the pantomimic conventions of ballet-
dancers.

A similar contrast is observed in literature. As
there are occasionally actors who *personate*—who give
expression to a genuine feeling—so there are occasionally writers, not merely littérateurs, who give
expression in words to the actual thought which is in
their minds. The writer uses words which are conventional signs, but he uses them with a sincerity and
directness of individual expression which makes them
the genuine utterance of *his* thoughts and feelings;
the littérateur uses conventional phrases, but he uses
them without the guiding instinct of individual expression; he tries to express what others have
expressed, not what is really in his own mind. With
a certain skill, the littérateur becomes an acceptable
workman; but we never speak of him as a *writer*,
never estimate him as a man of genius, unless he can
make his own soul speak to us. The conventional
language of poetry and passion, of dignity and drollery, may be more or less skilfully used by a writer of
talent; but he never delights us with those words
which come from the heart, never thrills us with the
simple touches of nature—those nothings which are
immense, and which make writing memorable.

In saying that Ristori is a conventional actress,
therefore, I mean that with great art she employs the
traditional conventions of the stage, and reproduces

the effects which others have produced, but does not deeply move us, because not herself deeply moved. Take away her beauty, grace, and voice, and she is an ordinary comedian; whereas Schröder, Devrient, and Pasta were assuredly neither handsome nor imposing in physique; and Rachel made a common Jewish physiognomy lovely by mere force of expression. In Medea Ristori was conventional and admirable. In Adrienne she was conventional and inartistic; for while the character was not *personated*, but simulated, it was simulated by conventional signs drawn from a totally wrong source. The comedy was the comedy of a *soubrette;* the playfulness had the *minauderie* of a frivolous woman, not the charm of a smile upon a serious face. It is a common mistake of conventional serious actors in comic scenes to imitate the "business" and manner of comic actors. The actor of serious style wishing to be funny thinks he must approach the low comedy style, and is often vulgar, always ineffective, by his very efforts at being effective. Ristori might have learned from Rachel that the lighter scenes of Adrienne could be charming without once touching on the "business" of the *soubrette;* and play-goers who remember Helen Faucit, especially in parts like Rosalind (a glimpse of which was had the other night), will remember how perfectly that fine actress can represent the joyous playfulness of young animal spirits, without once ceasing to be poetical. The gaiety of a serious nature even in its excitement must always preserve a certain tone which distinguishes it from the mirth of unimpassioned natures; a certain ground-swell of emotion should be felt beneath. The manner may be light, but it should spring from a deep nature : it is the difference between the comedy of Shakspeare or Molière, even when most extravagant, and the comedy of Congreve or Scribe; there may be a heartier laugh, but it has a more serious background. At any rate, the unity of effect which is demanded in all representation is greatly damaged when, as in the case of Adrienne represented by Ristori, instead of the playfulness of an impassioned woman, we have a patchwork of effects—a bit of a *soubrette* tacked on to a bit of the coquette, that again to a bit of the *ingénue*, and that to a tragic part. Ristori was not one woman in several moods, but several actresses playing several scenes.

Nevertheless, while insisting on her deficiencies, I must repeat the expression of my admiration for Ristori as a distinguished actress; if not of the highest rank, she is very high, in virtue of her personal gifts, and the trained skill with which these gifts are applied. And her failures are instructive. The failures of distinguished artists are always fruitful in suggestion. The question naturally arises, why is her success so great in certain plays, and so dubious in Shakspeare or the drama? It is of little use to say that Lady Macbeth and Adrienne are beyond her means; that is only restating the fact; can we not trace both success and failure to one source? In what is called the ideal drama, constructed after the Greek type, she would be generally successful, because the simplicity of its motives and the artificiality of its structure, removing it from beyond the region of or-

dinary experience, demand from the actor a corresponding artificiality. Attitudes, draperies, gestures,
tones, and elocution which would be incongruous in a
drama approaching more nearly to the evolutions of
ordinary experience, become, in the ideal drama,
artistic modes of expression; and it is in these that
Ristori displays a fine selective instinct, and a rare felicity of organization. All is artificial, but then all is
congruous. A noble unity of impression is produced.
We do not demand individual truth of character and
passion; the ideal sketch suffices. It is only on a
smaller scale what was seen upon the Greek stage,
where the immensity of the theatre absolutely inter-
dicted all individualizing; spectators were content with
masks and attitudes where in the modern drama we
demand the fluctuating physiognomy of passion, and
the minute individualities of character.

When, however, the conventional actress descends
from the ideal to the real drama, from the simple and
general to the complex and individual in personation,
she is at a disadvantage. Rachel could make this
descent, as all will remember who saw her Adrienne
or Lady Tartufe; but then Rachel *personated,* she
spoke through the character, she suffered her inward
feelings to express themselves in outward signs; she
had not to cast about her for the outward signs which
conventionally expressed such feelings. She had but
a limited range, there were few parts she could play:
but those few she personated, those she created. I
do not think that Ristori could personate; she would
always seek the conventional signs of expression,

although frequently using them with consummate skill.

If what I have said is true, it is clear that the gain to our stage from the study of such an actress would be small. Her beauty, her distinction, her grace, her voice, are not imitable; and nowhere does she teach the actor to rely on natural expression. Still more is this the case with Fechter, an artist many degrees inferior to Ristori, yet an accomplished actor in his own sphere. With regard to Mdlle. Stella Colas, bad as our actors are, they have nothing to learn from her. As I said, she is very pretty, and has a powerful voice: but her performance of Juliet, which seems to delight so many honest spectators, is wholly without distinction. During the first two acts one recognizes a well-taught pupil, whose by-play is very good, and whose youth and beauty make a pleasant scenic illusion. The balcony scene, though not at all representing Shakspeare's Juliet, was a pretty and very effective bit of acting. It was mechanical, but skilful too. It assured me that she was not an actress of any spontaneity; but it led me to hope more from the subsequent scenes than she did effect. Indeed, as the play advanced, my opinion of her powers sank. No sooner were the stronger emotions to be expressed than the mediocrity and conventionalism became more salient. She has great physical energy, and the groundlings are delighted with her displays of it; nor does the monotony of her vehemence seem to weary them, more than the inartistic redundance of effort in the quieter scenes. She has not yet learned to speak a speech, but tries to make every *line* emphatic. Partly this may be due to the difficulty of pronouncing a foreign language; but not wholly so, as is shown in the redundancy of gesture and "business." Her elocution would be very defective in her own language; and its least defect, to my apprehension, is the imperfection of her English accent. With all her vehemence, she is destitute of passion; she "splits the ears of the groundlings," but moves no human soul. Her looks, tones, gestures—all have the well-known melodramatic unreality; and if a British public riotously applauds her energetic passages, it is but justice to that public to say that it *also* applauds the ranting Romeo, and other amazing representatives of the play.

With regard to the young actress herself about whom I am forced to speak thus harshly, I see so much *material* for future distinction that I almost regret this early success. So much personal charm, so much energy, and so much ambition, may even yet carry her to the front ranks; but at present, I believe that every French critic would be astonished at the facility with which English audiences have accepted his young countrywoman; and he would probably make some derogatory remarks upon our insular taste. I do not for one moment deny her success—I only point to its moral. The stage upon which such acting could be regarded as excellent is in a pitiable condition. It is good mob acting, charming the eye and stunning the ear. The audiences have for so long been unused to see any truer or more refined representation, that they may be excused if, misled by the public press, and the prestige attached to the young

French woman because she is French, they go prepared to see something wonderful, and believe that a
Juliet so unlike anything they have ever seen is really
a remarkable representation. The applauders find
their more intelligent friends unwilling to admit that
Mdlle. Colas is at present anything more than a very
pretty woman, and peevishly exclaim, "Hang it! you
are so difficult to please." But I believe that, were
the stage in a more vigorous condition, there would
be no difference of opinion on this point. If Mdlle.
Colas finds easy admirers, it is because, as the Spaniards say, in the kingdom of the blind the one-eyed
is king.

CHAPTER XII.

THE DRAMA IN PARIS. 1865.

AS the critic's office is somewhat of a sinecure just now in London, the suggestion of a visit to the Paris theatres naturally arises in the mind of one desirous of writing something about the art of acting. The present condition of the English drama is deplored by all lovers of the art. It is the more irritating because never were theatres so flourishing. A variety of concurrent causes, which need not here be enumerated, has reduced the stage to its present pitiable condition. We have many theatres nightly crowded by an eager but uncritical public, and no one theatre in which a critical public can hope to enjoy a tolerable performance. I have a friend who maintains that the performances are good enough for the audiences. But he is cynical. Without impeaching the justice of his contempt, there is a restriction to be made. The masses crowding the theatres may, perhaps, care for nothing better than what is given them; yet there is a smaller public—choice in its tastes, and large enough to support a theatre—which would eagerly welcome a fine actor or a well-written drama.

Unhappily art is not like commerce, delicately sen-sitive to the laws of demand and supply.

There is abundance of bad acting to be seen in Paris, as elsewhere; and bad acting, like bad writing, has a remarkable uniformity, whether seen on the French, German, Italian, or English stage: it all seems modeled after two or three types, and those the least like types of good acting. The fault gen-erally lies less in the bad imitation of a good model, than in the successful imitation of a bad model. The style of expression is not simply conventional, the conventionality is absurdly removed from truth and grace. The majority have not learned to speak, much less to act: they mouth and gabble, look at the audience instead of their interlocutors, fling emphasis at random, mistake violence for emotion, grimace for humor, and express their feelings by signs as conven-tional and as unlike nature as the gestures of a ballet-dancer. Good acting, on the contrary, like good writing, is remarkable for its individuality. It charms by its truth; and truth is always original. It has certain qualities which, belonging to the funda-mental excellences of the art, are common—such as distinctness and quiet power in elocution, *gradation* in expression, and ruling calmness, which is never felt as coldness, but keeps the artist master of his effects; yet these qualities have in each case the individual stamp of the actor, and seem to belong only to him.

Specimens of both bad and good are to be seen in perfection at the Théâtre Français. Indeed, were it not for a few remarkable exceptions which keep up the traditional standard of excellence, one would fear that the Théâtre Français was also sinking to the level of general mediocrity, and that there also the art was dying out. Even the traditions of the stage seem departing. Elocution and deportment seem no longer indispensable elements. Of old there was perhaps a somewhat pedantic fastidiousness in these matters; but the error was an error on the right side. At present the absence of formality is supplied by a familiarity which is not grace. Purity of elocution was in itself a charm, especially when the exquisite language of Molière had to be spoken. A certain stately courtesy and elaborate formality suited the old comedy. The modern actors have become less artificial without becoming more natural. Tragedy ceased with Rachel. Comedy has still Regnier, Got, Provost, and Madame Plessy, but who is to replace them?

I saw three of Molière's comedies, " Georges Dandin, " " Tartufe," and " Le Mariage Forcé," with the greater part of " L'Amphitryon "; and with the exception of Regnier, Provost, and Madame Plessy, saw in them nothing that was not either bad or mediocre. Georges Dandin and Sganarelle were played by M. Talbot, whom I saw last year in " L'Avare," and whose performance of that part excited in me the liveliest desire—to see him no more. That the Théâtre Français can be reduced to such a pass as to have no better actor for this important class of characters is significant of the present condition of the stage. In London we might as well see Mr. Cullenford play Sir Peter Teazle. Again, for Tartufe we had Bressant, an excellent actor in his own line, but as unfit for Tartufe as Charles Mathews is for Iago. It was Bressant's first appearance in the part; and the idea of this handsome, elegant *jeune premier* playing the demure sensual hypocrite, was in itself a curiosity. I must do him the justice to say that curiosity was the sole emotion excited. A more complete failure I have seldom seen made by a good actor; but it was a failure from which actors might learn a valuable lesson, were not the lesson so often taught in vain: namely, the necessity of restricting themselves to parts for which they have the *physical* qualifications. Acting being personation, it is clear that unless the actor has the personal qualifications requisite for the representation of the character, no amount of ability in conceiving the part will avail. The Parisian critics who wrote in such raptures of Bressant's performance can hardly— if they were sincere—have understood this.

The part of Tartufe admits of various representations. Molière has sketched the character in such broad and general outlines, vigorous, yet wanting in detail, that the actor is free to fill up these outlines in several ways without endangering verisimilitude. Tartufe may be one of those hypocrites whose fat hands, flabby cheeks, oystery eyes, and unctuous manners give them an air of comfortable sensualism and greasy piety, very odious, but very comic; or he may be dark, saturnine, lean, lank, and harsh. He may be demure and velvety in his cat-like motions, or severe with a suppressed consciousness of his virtue and your wickedness. He may have thin lips or lustful eyes, cringing humility or hard unfeelingness. But Bressant is by nature excluded from the presentation of any of these types. He did not show any indication of having vividly felt the character at all, and was wholly incompetent to present it. His appearance and manner were those of a handsome young curate who has committed a forgery and cannot conceal his anxiety at the coming exposure. His love-making had excellent points if considered as the love-making of a young *roué*, but was utterly unlike the love-making of a Tartufe. When he says, in extenuation—

> Ah ! pour être dévot je n'en suis pas moins homme ;
> Et lorsqu'on vient à voir vos celestes appas
> Un cœur se laisse prendre et ne raisonne pas.
> Je sais qu'un tel discours de moi paroît étrange,
> Mais, madame, après tout je ne suis pas un ange,

he threw great persuasive fervor into his voice and manner, but he completely dropped the *persona* of Tartufe, and assumed that of Lovelace. Then, again, when, trying to reassure Elmire, he says—

> Mais les gens comme nous brûlent d'un feu discret,
> Avec qui, pour toujours, on est sûr du secret,

there was nothing of the oily rascality and sanctified security which the words demanded. He promised her—

> De l'amour sans scandale et du plaisir sans peur,

with a fervor which had no touch of hypocrisy in it. When he is betrayed to Orgon, and artfully confronts his accuser by accusing himself of being a mass of

infamy and vice, there was no twang in his tone, no
artful assertion of innocence in his manner: the
comedy of the situation was altogether missed.

The only actors I have seen in the part of Tartufe
are Bocage and our Webster.   Bocage was saturnine
and sensual, Webster was cat-like and sensual: both
were forcible, both were true.   Bressant was feeble,
and completely out of his element.   Were it not for
that strange ambition which prompts actors to attempt fine parts because the parts are fine, and not
because the actors have the requisite representative
qualities, it would have been inexplicable that an
actor like Bressant should for a moment have desired
to play Tartufe.

The performance of "Tartufe," on the whole, was
by no means admirable.   Provost, a really fine actor,
was very humorous as Orgon, though somewhat too
bourgeois, both in appearance and manner.   Madame
Plessy, as Elmire, spoke the verses with exquisite
ease, precision, and grace.   Hers is the perfection of
elocution, highly elaborated, yet only seen to be elaborated by critics who can also see its ease.   In her
one great scene, that in which she lures Tartufe to
disclose himself, she was very good.   But I cannot
give a word of praise to the rest; and considering the
claims of the Théâtre Francais, considering its reputation for producing the classic drama with minute
attention to the ensemble, it seemed to me as if here
also were visible the general signs of a decline of
the art.

The lively little comedy "Le Mariage Forcé" was
performed in a somewhat deadly-lively manner, ex-

cept in the one brief scene where Regnier appears as Doctor Pancrace. This scene, a capital satire on the scholastic doctors, which everyone has enjoyed in the reading, was played by Regnier with a *verve* and a comic verisimilitude perfectly delightful. His exuberance of fun never overstepped the line which separates comedy from farce. He was as extravagant as Molière, and as true. The hard stupidity which comes from pre-occupation, the pedantic self-sufficiency, and the irritable self-love were shown in their most ludicrous forms. The expression of his face, when he was *not* listening to what Sganarelle was saying, but, instead of listening, seemed framing a reply to his antagonist, was exquisitely humorous. It was a flash of humor which served to clear the air, when weariness was beginning to whisper "time for bed."

There may be two opinions respecting the performance of the classic drama at the Théâtre Français; there can be but one respecting the performance of modern comedy. If the traditions are dying out, if the rising actors are less rigorously trained or are less endowed by nature than were their predecessors, so that the idealism of dramatic art finds few successful cultivators, at any rate the realists are successful. To see such a performance as that of Emile Augier's last comedy, "Maître Guérin," revives one's faith in French acting. The comedy itself, like most of Augier's works, is serious rather than comic: the gaiety is the smile of the intellect, not the mirth of animal spirits, not the laugh which bubbles up at ludicrous images. It contains some admirable writing, and one or two piquant sayings. The interest is progressive. The characters, though faintly sketched, are well contrasted. But the piece requires very fine acting, and would not bear transplantation to our stage.

In the first act we are introduced to a young and brilliant coquette, Madame Lecoutellier, played by Madame Plessy, who has a rich old husband and a spendthrift young nephew. She likes the old man's money, but winces under the galling yoke of his name; *née* Valtaneuse, as she delights to sign herself, she is forced to submit to be called Lecoutellier, which, for a woman of fashion with mundane instincts highly developed, is not pleasant. Her hope is to be able to purchase the estate of Valtaneuse, which once belonged to her family, and which is now the last remnant of the property of M. Desroncerets, a philanthropist, who has squandered a fortune on his inventions, and who has given his daughter the absolute management of his affairs, so that he may be saved from ruining himself by further attempts at immortalizing his name and enriching his country. The idea of this situation is an excellent one: we have the passionate devotion of the old man contrasted with the unusual good sense and severity of his daughter, forced into business habits and restrictive prudence, obliged to deny her father the indulgence of dreams which would be his ruin, obliged to seem hard and unfeminine out of her very tenderness and care for him. But the situation has been too imperfectly wrought out. It might have made the subject of a piece. M. Augier has made it a mere episode.

Although Desroncerets has dispossessed himself of his property, no sooner does a new scheme present itself than he borrows money on the sly. Maître Guérin, the country lawyer, is ready to purchase the estate of Valtaneuse (by means of a man of straw) at much less than its value ; and Desroncerets raises a hundred thousand francs in this way by a secret sale, with power to repurchase at the end of a year. He has no fears of being unable to repurchase it—what inventor ever doubts the future?—and with the money thus raised he is confident of earning a million. There is something sad and comic in the scene, which was played throughout by Got (Maître Guérin) in a marvellous manner. When I first read the piece I was unable to detect in Maître Guérin the material for a fine part : all is so faintly indicated, and so meagre in detail, that the actor has the whole onus thrown upon him of creating a part. No sooner did Got make his appearance than it was clear we were going to witness an original and powerful creation. His make-up, gait, look, and manner were such as would have thrown Balzac into ecstacies. There was no mistaking the type. There was no doubt as to the intense individuality of that knowing, scheming, vulgar, respectable bourgeois — so prosaic, so hard, yet so respectable ! The very man to be trusted and respected ; the man certain to get on ; certain never to offend prejudices, nor to overstep the limits of law.

This Guérin has a son, a distinguished young officer, the soul of honor, very unlike his father, who, not understanding, and rather despising him, nevertheless schemes for his advancement, as fathers with paternal egoism will scheme. Louis was formerly in love with Desroncerets' daughter, but her business habits and attention to money matters chilled his enthusiasm, and he is now entangled in the meshes of the coquettish Madame Lecoutellier. The scene between these two, which closes the act, is a masterly bit of comedy. He comes to bid her adieu on his departure for Mexico. She does not wish to lose him, though—coquette-like —she only wants him to dangle after her. She insinuates that if he joins his regiment he cannot care for her. He pleads his honor, which forbids his changing his regiment on the eve of a campaign. She suggests that her husband has influence enough to get him promoted. He replies coldly, "Your husband! Thank you, madame, but I do not choose to owe my promotion to anyone but myself, least of all to your husband." With an air of affected ignorance she asks him, "Why?" "You have forbidden me to say." "That's true; and I admire the scrupulous fidelity with which you obey orders!" "I treat the honor of others with the same respect as my own. You told me one day that to declare love to a married woman was as great an insult as to propose to a soldier to desert his standard." *"Perhaps I exaggerated a little!"* It is impossible to conceive the *finesse* with which Madame Plessy uttered these words. Indeed, her whole performance during this scene was enchanting. It was the quintessence of feminine wile. The pretty little *bouderie*, the provoking scepticism, the delicately yet plainly implied avowals, were enough to turn the head of a stronger man. Poor

Louis of course succumbs; carried away by the thought that she loves him, he passionately declares that he will at once quit the army. He leaves her horrified at the idea. She is afraid that having quitted the army for her sake, " il se croirait des droits,' which is precisely what the coquette will not permit. At this juncture the news arrives of the sudden death of her husband. She writes to Louis, " I am a widow; respect my year of mourning; depart, and do not write to me." She thus gains a year's delay; and "dans un an, tout ceci sera de l'histoire ancienne."

A year has elapsed at the opening of the second act. In that year Desroncerets has lost all his money; Madame Lecoutellier and her nephew have been to law about the will of the deceased Lecoutellier, and Louis Guérin has distinguished himself in the campaign, returning as colonel. Guérin, who finds himself on the eve of becoming possessor of Valtaneuse, tells his wife of his plans to marry Louis to Madame Lecoutellier. To render this possible he commences by diminishing the distance between the fortunes of the lady and his son. How? First, by persuading her to compromise the lawsuit with her nephew, and divide the property. Secondly, by tempting her with the château of Valtaneuse. A very comic scene occurs between the aunt and nephew, in which Guérin tries to persuade them to divide the property; an idea acceptable to both, were it not that they are so enraged with the aspersions of each other's advocates. Even this obstacle may be set aside, Arthur says, by their marrying each other. The disgust of Guérin at such a proposition (so subversive of all his plans) was excessively comic and wonderfully true. As he cannot openly oppose it, he resolves to frustrate it by stratagem. When she departs he pretends that she has dropped a letter. This letter is the one written to her by Louis a year before, but never delivered. It rouses Arthur's jealousy, as Guérin intended.

The third act is somewhat weaker than the others. The upshot of it is that Guérin proposes to Madame Lecoutellier that she should marry Louis, and thus become mistress of Valtaneuse, which he is about to possess. She consents. In the fourth act Desroncerets, unable to raise or borrow money, applies to his daughter for funds. She refuses. A powerful scene (very indifferently acted) occurs here, in which the loving daughter is forced to seem harsh, forced to disobey her father, forced at length to confess that he has spent all his money, and that for the last three years they have been living on her dowry.

The secret once disclosed, Louis, who turned from her because he thought her mercenary, now turns back again repentant to her feet. But he discovers the plan by which her father will be deprived of his only resource, the château of Valtaneuse. His sense of honor is justly outraged at such an act, and he feels called upon to prevent it. He does prevent it— pays back the money; maddens his father, who disinherits him; and marries Francine Desroncerets. The final scene of quarrel is very dramatic. Guérin is utterly baffled, and his rage is tragic-comical. Even his wife deserts him; she who, for five-and-thirty years, has been his patient victim, now raises her head, and declares her purpose of quitting the house with her son.   The author has not sufficiently prepared this—indeed, it is in contradiction with the spirit and language of the earlier scenes in which Madame Guérin speaks of her husband as the best of men, and seems devoted to him; nevertheless, it is a powerful dramatic incident; and when Guérin is left solitary, the solitude of selfishness is vividly indicated by his being reduced to ask the man of straw to stay and dine with him.

Nothing could be more natural or more suggestive than Got's acting of this part.   From first to last it was a study; and I can give our actors no better advice than to read the play, picture to themselves how they would perform the part of Guérin, and then go to Paris and carefully watch Got.   Such acting is worth the study of every artist, no matter what his line, because it exhibits vividly the singular effect which is produced by truthfulness.   Every gesture, every look, every tone of the actor seems instinct with the bourgeois nature.   The way he uses his handkerchief, the way he sits down, the smallest detail is prompted by an inward vision of the nature of the man represented.   Then, again, Madame Plessy, though, as a woman, without much charm, as an artist is well worth studying, not only because of the refined naturalness of her manner, but also on account of the exquisite skill of her execution.

The great difficulty in elocution is *to be* slow, and not to *seem* slow — to speak the phrases with such distinctness, and such management of the breath, that each shall tell, yet due proportion be maintained.

Hurry destroys the effect; and actors hurry because they dread, and justly dread, the heaviness of a slow utterance. The art is so to manage the time that it shall not appear slow to the hearer; and this is an art very rarely understood by actors. No sooner have they to express excitement or emotion of any kind than they seem to lose all mastery over the rhythm and cadence of their speech.* Let them study great speakers, and they will find that in passages which seem rapid there is a measured rhythm, and that even in the whirlwind of passion there is as strict a regard to *tempo* as in passionate music. *Resistent flexibility* is the perfection of elocution.

Comedy nobly justifies its existence when it dignifies amusement with a healthy, moral tendency, carrying a lesson in its laugh, a warning in its pictures. Too often the comedy of our day holds itself aloof from the realities of life, and seeks amusement in the fantastic combination of incidents and characters which have only a distant reference to the on-goings of society. Hence the common phrase,

* Sanson, the excellent professor of elocution, tells us how—

d'un mot plaisant, terrible, ou tendre
On double la valeur en le faisant attendre ;

a point well understood by the elder Kean, who, however, often allowed his pauses to degenerate into tricks. Sanson adds :

Tantôt l'agile voix se précipite et vole ;
Tantôt il faut savoir ralentir sa parole.
Ignorant de son art les plus vulgaires lois
Plus d'un acteur se laisse entraîner par sa voix ;
Sa rapide parole étourdit l'auditoire :
Il semble concourir pour un prix de mémoire.

"that is all very well on the stage:" thus the satire becomes harmless because felt to be fantastic; the moral is sterile because inapplicable.

In the comedy—or shall I not rather call it tragedy?—of "Les Lionnes Pauvres," by Emile Augier and E. Foussier, which was revived at the "Vaudeville" recently, and which, though wretchedly performed, was terribly affecting, the authors have shown us what comedy may be—should be. They have boldly laid bare one of the hideous sores of social life, and painted the consequences of the present rage for dress and luxury which is rapidly demoralizing the middle classes of Europe. No one who knows how severe is the struggle of families having small and fixed incomes, can contemplate without dismay the tendency of all classes to imitate the extravagance of the classes above them. What Goethe humorously says of literary aspirants, that no one is contented to be a cobbler, every one pretending to be a poet—

> Niemand will ein Schuster seyn ;
> Jedermann ein Dichter—

is true of social aspirants. We all belong to the aristocracy. If we cannot ride in our own carriages, we can wear dresses only meant to be worn in a carriage. If we cannot delude our friends into the belief that we are rich, we will do our best to delude strangers in the street. We may not be duchesses, but we will dress as like them as our means and imitations will permit. The crinoline disease corrupts all classes. The wife of a clerk whose salary is four pounds a week sweeps the dirt of the pavement with her silken train, and is neither dismayed by the uncleanliness nor ashamed of the extravagance;·if anyone mildly remonstrates on this wicked waste, she quietly answers, "They are worn so!" Such extravagance can only be supported by debts which end in dishonor, or by a pinching economy at home. The necessaries are sacrificed to the vanities. The husband and children suffer that the wife and mother may "make a figure"—which she doesn't. In Italy and France one hears it universally said that wives purchase their toilettes with the honor of their husbands. In England such an accusation would be indignantly repelled. Meanwhile even in England the excess of expenditure must be made up by a corresponding deficiency somewhere. "In France," say our authors, "as long as the wife remains virtuous, the husband pays twopence for a penny loaf. Then comes the time when he pays a penny for a twopenny loaf. She begins by robbing and ends by enriching the house." The husband is hoodwinked. He is in a state of chronic amazement at the progress of manufactures, the cheapness of silks, the marvels of "bargains" that are to be had by those who will spend one-half of their time in contriving their toilettes, and the other half in exhibiting them. He never suspects where all this splendor comes from, until he opens his eyes to his dishonor.

In "Les Lionnes Pauvres" this danger and this vice are painted with a firm, remorseless hand. Unhappily, the details are some of them such as would scarcely be tolerated on our stricter stage : but with that exception the comedy is worthy of the highest praise. It is badly acted by everyone except Felix, who plays the part of moral censor with charming ease and incisive effect. His art of branding vice with an epigram, and of uttering a moral while never for one moment committing the mistake of assuming the air of sermonizing superiority, could not be surpassed. The laughter left behind it a serious reflection. Take Felix away, however, and the performance is one which must make every Englishman pause to consider the justice of the popular opinion that the French stage is greatly superior to the English in the perfection of its *ensemble.* Indeed, that opinion seems to me to require revision. I do not speak of the Vaudeville only, but of the theatres in general. There are good actors, admirable actors, on the French stage : but a really good *ensemble* I saw but at one theatre—the Porte St. Martin—where the "Vingt Ans Après" of Dumas was played by Mélingue, Clarence, Lacressonière, Montal, and Mdlle. Duverger, in the principal parts, and very tolerable actors in the subordinate parts, presenting a combination such as we can make no claim to, and such as I did not see elsewhere rivaled. It will, of course, be understood that I do not place the Théâtre Français below the Porte St. Martin in absolute, but in relative merit. There are far better actors at the Théâtre Français ; and in "Maître Guérin" the *ensemble* was satisfactory. But the standard of that theatre is, in all respects, higher ; and in the performance of the classic drama it is certainly inferior to the performance of melodrama at the Porte St. Martin.

Altogether, my visit to this Boulevard theatre was very gratifying, and I could not help thinking what a gain it would be to our actors if they would go there and study the art. They would see that it was by no means necessary to outrage nature for the sake of effect; and that in the important matter of manage- ment of the voice much might be learned, especially that the simple inflexions of natural utterance were far more telling than the growls of the *voix de ventre*, or the surprising mouthings which with us are mis- taken for effective elocution. They would also see that attention to the business of the scenes could be given without thrusting themselves forward and overdoing their parts.

Not that these Porte St. Martin actors are irre- proachable. By no means. They, too, have their conventionalities and their shortcomings. But if they fall short of a high standard, they are, compared with what we are accustomed to see in England simple, natural, and excellent. One of them I am tempted to single out, partly because of the rare qualities of his performance, and partly because being a young actor who has not yet made a reputation, his name does not figure in large type beside that of Mélingue, Clarence and Lacressonière. It is no exaggeration to say that to see this young man, Montal, play the part of Mordaunt in "Vingt Ans Après," is worth a journey to Paris for any actor who is bent on master- ing some of the secrets of his art. On his very first appearance, as he stood silent in the background, there was no mistaking that an impressive actor was before us. He had the rare power of being silently eloquent; of standing quite still and yet riveting attention on him. I knew not who he was, and had never seen the play, yet felt at once that in the pale young monk standing on the stairs at the back of the stage, there was something boding and fateful. Much of this, of course, was due to the *physique* of the actor; but even actors who had no such nervous temperament and sharply-cut features might imitate the quietness and significance of his gestures. As the play proceeded, it became evident that his range of expression was limited, and that he could not adequately represent emotion in its higher forms; but terror, sarcasm, sombre scheming, and serpentine adroitness were admirably expressed by him. So effective were his make up, gestures, looks, and manners, that on quitting the theatre, and for many days afterwards, my imagination was haunted by the vision.

The heroine was played by Mdlle. Duverger, interesting to me as the actress whom it was understood we were shortly to see on the London boards, in accordance with that surprising fashion of importing foreigners which the success of Fechter has introduced. The fashion is not complimentary to our public taste. Is it that we have been so tolerant of laxity in the matter of elocution, and have shown so little fastidiousness as to how our noble language was spoken, that managers believed we should not wince at the strange caprices of foreign accent and rhythm? A few years ago the public would not accept Miss Smithson (now Madame Berlioz) because of her Irish accent; yet Fechter, Mdlle. Stella Colas, and Mdlle. Beatrice have found enthusiastic admirers. In a little

while we may rival even the Germans in endurance.
They listened without protest to the negro actor,
Aldridge, declaiming "Othello" in English while all
the other characters spoke German. And the Germans, we constantly hear are ' a nation of critics!

As we were to have Mdlle. Duverger in England I
watched her performance with some curiosity One
excellent quality she undoubtedly has: fine eyes. If
you ask me, What are her talents as an actress? my
answer is, She has fine eyes. A pretty woman has
always the talent of being pretty; and the mass of
play-goers in our day demand little more. How Mdlle.
Duverger may manage to fill certain parts with beauty
and costume we must wait to see; but of this much I
am assured by the one performance I witnessed, that,
as an actress, she is thoroughly conventional, and not
impressive in her conventionality.

I have been instructing myself in Christian mythol-
ogy as presented on the French stage. Not even the
heat nor the tumult of a popular theatre could keep
me from "Paradise Lost" at the Gaité; the attraction of the fall of the angels, pandemonium, Adam
and Eve, the death of Abel, the children of Cain, and
the deluge, was irresistible. You can with ease imagine the kind of boulevard poetry and religious
sentiment, *un peu fort de café*, which a melodramatic
spectacle on this theme would produce; but there
were points in the performance which you could not
have imagined—at least, which I could not—and that

serves the turn of my sentence quite as well. You may have pictured to yourself the rebel angels personated by a dozen supers in dresses of no particular period· you may have imagined a stout ballet-girl in very scant clothing representing Eve; a well-shaved Adam in skins and fleshings: and a Cain with hair and beard trimmed in the latest style· but I deny that you could have conceived a Satan so jovial and grotesque — such a compound of Falstaff turned acrobat and a First Murderer dreaming of "leading business"! It is no exaggeration to say that I was quite haunted all yesterday by the vision of that fat man in scaly costume representing the serpent, a tempter with the sort of fat elasticity of bearing which we sometimes observe in the French Banting —"caught young." What the authors had put into his mouth was sufficiently grotesque and eminently French, especially where Satan makes love to Eve, and, on being repulsed by that matron, kneels at her feet and weeps in the approved style: "Satan à tes pieds! Satan pleure!" says the tempter—as if that must be irresistible!

The audience seemed intensely interested, not only in this love-making, but in every other scene of the great mythic drama; and when Eve tries to awaken the better feelings of Cain, and appeals to him as a *bourgeoise* mother would appeal to her refractory son (on the stage), recalling the early years of maternal solicitude and maternal anguish, the women around me were incessantly wiping their eyes, and the men before me were deeply interested. There were, indeed, a few sceptical young men who seemed only impressed by the ludicrous aspect of the actors or the scenes. But the mass of the audience evidently accepted this mystery-play of the nineteenth century with as much seriousness as their ancestors in the fourteenth century accepted the naïve representations of Biblical stories which their priests furnished in good faith. And *this* constituted the real interest of the performance to me. This was one of the points which I had not been prepared for. Yet while I saw the seriousness of the people in presence of a singularly vulgar and unimaginative reproduction of one of the grand stories of human destiny, and thought of the shock such a presentation would give to the feelings of Protestants in what they would irresistibly feel to be a degradation of the mysteries of religion, I could not help recognizing that the Catholic audience, especially the lower classes, would have been so prepared from infancy by what they daily saw in their churches and cathedrals, that the idea of any irreverence or of any vulgarization would not occur to them. After the images they had worshipped from childhood, the aspect of the Angel Michael, with a flaming sword and superb wings, announcing to Satan that the Creator had just endowed the universe with the earth, *délicieux séjour*, as he said, for the new favorite, Man, the stage must have seemed the more imposing of the two. And, probably, their imaginations of the flight of Cain had never pictured anything so picturesquely awful as the tableaux which here reproduced on a large scale the picture by Prudhon one does *not* admire in the gallery of the Louvre.

It was not for the acting that I went to the Gaîté.

I had seen Dumaine, the hero of this house, as
N. T. Hicks used to be of the transpontine theatres,
and did not anticipate that his performance of Satan
would be striking, though it proved, as I said, im-
mensely droll.   But I did expect that Montal would
have made something of Cain.   Montal some months
ago played the villain in "Vingt Ans Après," and
made one feel before he spoke that he was an evil influence; I was therefore curious to see him in another
kind of part.   Alas! as Cain he showed no good
quality.   It was an ungrateful part to play, and he
played it ungratefully.   He was violent, ill at ease,
conventional.   But he was surpassed in badness by
Clarence, who used to be an excellent *jeune premier*, and who as Adam gave a ludicrous illustration
of what the coat-and-waistcoat style of acting comes
to when it has to deal with anything more elevated.

Yet the effect of the story, so impressive in its religious associations, and so interesting to the universal heart in its human suggestions, aided by a
splendid spectacle, has made this very prosaic and
absurd piece, in spite of the acting, one of the great
successes of the year.   The house is crowded every
night.   With us the Lord Chamberlain would not
even permit the title to appear on the bills; and
even if there were no licenser of plays, the public
would tear up the benches at the opening scene of
the fall of the angels, so profound would be the
agitation of horror at the sight of what would seem
this daring desecration of things sacred.   To the
French it is anything but blasphemous; and we
make a great mistake in supposing that there is

not as much good honest religious feeling in France
as in England, though it may take a different shape

To this account I will add the notice of a profess-
edly religious performance of a dramatic kind, given
not in Paris, but in Antwerp. The contrast is as great
as might be excepted from the two cities.

Antwerp is delightful by day when the churches
are open and the gallery is to be enjoyed; but
Antwerp at night, after you have well explored its
streets and know its architecture, is not an eminently
amusing city. There are men who can sit in a café,
or smoke and dawdle through the postprandial hours,
and be content. I am less easily contented, and
whenever I am away from my own hearth-rug,
the shades of evening bring with them a restless
desire for music or dramatic entertainment. At
Antwerp there was nothing of the kind. Not
even my desire for amusement could be cheated
with the dreary performance of an equestrian troop,
foreseen to be a spectacle of bony women jumping
through hoops, and hideous men vaulting on and off
horses, to the sounds of a most brassy band. I
preferred the hotel.

What, then, was my agitation of delight when,
restlessly reading everything like a placard which
promised performance of one thing or another, I
came upon a huge bill, headed "Théâtre des
Variétés," setting forth that a performance of the
Ober-Ammergau mystery-play on the life and death
of our Saviour would take place on the Sunday? A
theatre seemed a strange place for this religious per-

formance (Groote Godsdienstige Voorstelling), and I had always imagined that the Ober-Ammergau peasants performed in the open air. Nevertheless the chance of seeing this spectacle—the last lingering remains of the mediæval drama, when plays were played in churches, and the actors were priests—was so exciting that I rushed off immediately after breakfast to secure places, without any regard to congruity.

Such a performance was indeed in all respect exceptional. A dingy little theatre, where one would expect to see broad farces and bloody melodramas, was to be the scene of a mimic representation of the most solemn and affecting of stories—a story so sacred that to Protestant feeling there is something shocking in the idea of its being brought into the remotest relation with anything like amusement, especially theatrical amusement. And, nevertheless, I believe that any Protestant who could have overcome the first repulsion would have witnessed the performance not only with deep interest but with the acknowledgment that it was really religious. Certain it is that on the Catholic audience assembled there the effect was purely that of religious awe and sympathetic interest. I am sorry to be obliged to add that the effect was transitory. Each scene was witnessed with hushed and engrossed attention; but as the curtain fell the spectators relapsed into gabble, laughter, and eatables, as if they were indeed "at the play." This rather irritated me at the time; but now I bethink me that good Protestants may be seen coming out of church after listening to a most edifying discourse respecting the next world, and yet be chattering about the affairs of this world with lively levity.

Now as to the performance. It represented, in eighteen *tableaux vivants,* the most symbolic incidents in the sacred life, from the Nativity to the Resurrection. There being only pantomimic action, and no speaking, the dangers of vulgarizations or of ludicrous suggestion were avoided. The organ played during each scene and helped to deepen the impression. The stage was arrayed with black baize at the wings and back, thus forming a dark background against which the figures stood in relief. Occasionally a tree or seat occupied the foreground. The dresses were such as one usually sees in small provincial theatres, and the wigs and beards were especially rude. At first I feared the performance was going to be painfully childish in its attempts at illusion; for in the "Adoration of the Shepherds" there was a large doll lamb which baa'd when the boy pulled down its head—an attempt at realism which promised ill for what was to come. The pretty picture which followed—"The Flight into Egypt"—showed us Mary on a pasteboard donkey, with the infant in her arms; and the child had been taught to open his arms and bless the world, and to kiss his mother, with very touching simplicity. After this the performance was really remarkable in as far as it depended on the Christ—a tall and very handsome man, with noble and gentle bearing, who is said to prepare himself for the performance by weeks of prayer and meditation, and to suffer greatly from exhaustion when the excitement of acting is over. The others were all as bad as bad could be; but he was affecting. The adieu to his mother and friends at Bethany, the agony in the garden, the bearing of the cross, and meeting with Veronica, tasked his powers of mimic expression severely, and showed him to be in earnest or to be a great artist. The shudder of horror which ran through the house when the soldier smote him on the cheek proved how thorough was the imaginative belief of the audience. Never once throughout the long and varied scenes did he "drop the mask" and pass out of the character he had assumed. His action was fluent and unconventional, his face highly and variously expressive.

Many of the tableaux were imitated from celebrated pictures. Leonardo da Vinci of course was followed in the "Last Supper." The "Descent from the Cross" was copied from Rubens; the entombment and resurrection from various old pictures; the denial of Peter was excellently managed, but I could not recall any especial original for it.

On the whole, I came away satisfied that the effect of such performances was wholly beneficial. The common mind can only be impressed by visible symbols; and when these symbols are associated with primitive emotions, their influence is religious. Nothing can be more unlike this "Godsdienstige Voorstelling" than the audacious spectacle of "Le Paradis Perdu," where Satan made love to Eve in the style of a French novelist, and Eve had the most painful resemblance to a ballet-girl. Here at Antwerp, if a critical taste would have found many things to alter, it would have found none that were even remotely

injurious to the public mind.   Had the audience
showed a little hypocrisy, and pretended that the
performance had not only deeply moved them, but
had solemnized their thoughts for a while, I should
have been wholly pleased; but the audience, to their
credit be it said, had no thought of pretence in the
matter.

CHAPTER XIII.

THE DRAMA IN GERMANY. 1867.

THE drama is everywhere in Europe and America rapidly passing from an art into an amusement, just as of old it passed from a religious ceremony into an art. Those who love the drama cannot but regret the change, but all must fear that it is inevitable when they reflect that the stage is no longer the amusement of the cultured few, but the amusement of the uncultured and miscultured masses, and has to provide larger and lower appetites with food. For one play-goer who can appreciate the beauty of a verse, the delicate humor of a conception, or the exquisite adaptation of means to ends which gives ease and harmony to a work of art, there are hundreds who, insensible to such delights, can appreciate a parody, detect a pun, applaud a claptrap phrase of sentiment, and be exhilarated by a jingle and a dance; for one who can recognize, and, recognizing, can receive exquisite pleasure from, fine acting, thousands can appreciate costumes, bare necks, and " powerful ' grimace; thus the mass, easily pleased and liberally paying for the pleasure, rules the hour.

Unless a frank recognition of this inevitable tendency cause a decided separation of the drama which aims at art from those theatrical performances which only aim at amusement of a lower kind (just as classical music keeps aloof from all contact and all rivalry with comic songs and sentimental ballads), and unless this separation take place in a decisive restriction of one or more theatres to the special performances of comedy and the poetic drama, the final disappearance of the art is near at hand. It may be a question whether any capital in Europe could now sustain a theatre appealing only to the intellectual classes; and it may also be a question whether dramatists and actors could be found competent and willing to supply the art, could the audiences be secured. I do not venture to answer these questions: the more so because I am not insensible to the many and serious obstacles in the way of establishing such a theatre; but considering the really large numbers of cultivated minds, and the fascination to all minds of dramatic representation; considering further the pecuniary success of the Monday Popular Concerts in a city which tolerates German brass bands and resounds with nigger melodies, it is no extravagant hope that audiences might be found if adequate performances were offered. Not perhaps the crowds which enable a "sensation piece" to run two hundred nights,* or a burlesque to make the fortune of a theatre: but it should be remembered that if the audiences would be less numerous, the expenses of the theatre would

---

* Since then "The School for Scandal" has run for 200 nights, and "Hamlet" also for 200 nights.

also be proportionately small. It is only by a rigid adherence to the principle of specialization that such a scheme could have a chance. The theatre must be mounted with the sole purpose of performing works of art, for an art-loving public. It must avoid spectacle, scenic "effects," and encroachments on the domains of melodrama and burlesque; as quartet concerts avoid the attractions of military bands and comic songs. It must have one small company of well-trained and art-loving actors (what a condition!), not a large miscellaneous company attempting *all* kinds of performance.

Something like what is here indicated may be found in the Théâtre Français of Paris, and the Hof Theater in each of the German capitals. To be candid, one must add that none of these establishments are able to dispense with government assistance; they are not paying speculations; and if examination or experiment should prove that in the nature of the case such establishments could not be made to pay— if there is in England really no public large enough to support such an undertaking well managed—then we have nothing but to resign ourselves to the inevitable destruction of the drama; for certainly no English government would ever think of contributing a penny towards the elevation or the preservation of dramatic art.

In the course of a few weeks' ramble in Germany this summer I had but rare opportunities of ascertaining the present condition of the dramatic art, although during the last thirty years I have from time to time been fortunate enough to see most of the best actors Germany has produced. Now, as of old, there is a real respect for the art, both in the public and in the actors ; and at each theatre we see that striving after an *ensemble* so essential to the maintenance of the art, but which everywhere else except at the Théâtre Français is sacrificed to the detestable star system.   In Germany we may see actors of the first eminence playing parts which in England and America would be contemptuously rejected by actors of third-rate rank; and the "condescension," so far from lowering the favorite in the eyes of the public, helps to increase his favor.   I remember when Emil Devrient, then a young man, came to play Hamlet at Berlin, as a "guest," the great tragedian Seydelmann (the *only* great tragedian in my opinion that Germany has had during the last quarter of a century*) undertook the part of Polonius.   It was one of those memorable performances which mark an epoch in the play-goer's life.   Such a revelation of the character, and such *maestria* of execution, one can hardly hope to see again.   Had he played Laertes (and he would doubtless have consented to play it had there been any advantage in his doing so), he would still have been the foremost figure of the piece. At any rate he would have been the great actor, and the favorite of the Berliners.

And here it is only fair to add, in extenuation of the English actor's resistance against sacrificing his *amour propre* to the general good, that if he obsti-

---

* Mr. Schütz Wilson has just published an interesting "Glance at the German Stage," in which there is a sketch of Seydelmann.

nately declines to appear in a part unworthy of his
powers or his rank in the profession, he does so because, over and above the natural dislike of appearing
to some disadvantage, he knows in the first place that
the English public cares little for an *ensemble*, and in
the second place that the majority of the audience
will only see him in that unworthy part, and consequently will form an erroneous idea of his capabilities.
It is otherwise with the German actor. He knows
that the public expects and cares for an *ensemble*, and
he desires the general success of the performance, as
each individual in an orchestra desires that the
orchestral effect should be perfect. He knows,
moreover, that the same people who to-night see him
in an inferior part saw him last week, or will see him
next week, in the very best parts of his repertory.
He has, therefore, little to lose and much to gain by
playing well an inferior part. Further, his payment
is usually regulated by the times of performance.

Be the reasons what they may, the result is that
always at a German Hof Theater one is sure of the
very best *ensemble* that the company can present; and
one will often receive as much pleasure from the performance of quite insignificant parts as from the
leading parts on other stages. The actors are thoroughly *trained :* they know the principles of their art
—a very different thing from knowing " the business"! They pay laudable attention to one supremely
important point recklessly disregarded on our stage,
namely elocution. They know how to *speak*—both
verse and prose: to speak without mouthing, yet
with effective cadence; speech elevated above the

tone of conversation without being stilted. How
many actors are there on our stage who have learned
this? How many are there who suspect the mysterious charm which lies in rhythm, and have mastered its
music? How many are there who, with an art which
is not apparent except to the very critical ear, can
manage the cadences and emphases of prose, so as to
be at once perfectly easy, natural, yet incisive and
effective? The foreigner, whose ear has been somewhat lacerated by the dreadful intonations of common
German speech, is surprised to find how rich and
pleasant the language is when spoken on the stage;
the truth being that the actors have learned to speak,
and are not permitted to call themselves actors at a
Hof Theater until they have conquered those slovenly
and discordant intonations which distort the speech
of vulgar men. I was made more than ever sensible of this refinement of elocution by having passed
some weeks in a retired watering-place wholly inhab-
ited by Germans of the tradesman class, whose voices
and intonations so tormented me that I began to
think the most hideous sound in nature was the
cackle of half-a-dozen German women. To hear the
women on the stage after *that* was like hearing
singing after a sermon.

Next to excellence of elocution, which forms the
basis of good acting, comes the excellence of *miming*
—the expression of character. There are three great
divisions of mimetic art: first, the ideal and passionate; secondly, the humorous realism of comedy; and
lastly, the humorous idealism of farce. In the first and
last divisions the German stage seems poorly supplied

at present. But in the second division there is much excellence. And I remember this to have been always the case : tragic or poetic actors are rare, their power over the emotions fitful, but comic actors are abundant, though seldom successful in the riotously and fantastically humorous. Now precisely in this division, wherein Germany displays greatest power, England has at all times been most feeble. There has, indeed, of late years, arisen a certain ambition on the part of actors, and a demand on the part of certain audiences, which may be said to be leading our drama into the region of humorous realism and high comedy; nor is it without significance that this movement should have been coincident with an almost complete extinction of the passionate and ideal drama; but without making invidious mention of a few exceptions, it is simple justice to say that the efforts of our stage in this direction are but trivial beside the German, and men with us gain a reputation as "natural actors" for mimetic qualities which would be quite ordinary in Berlin, Dresden, Vienna, or Weimar.

One excellence noticeable on the German stage is the presentation of character in its individual traits, with just that amount of accentuation which suffices to make it incisive and laughable, yet restrains it from running over into extravagance and unreality. The performance at Berlin of a French comedy, "The Secret Agent," was an example.

The piece itself is lively and pleasant, with no eminent qualities, and happily without any French poison —sentimental or sensual. A young German duke has

come to the throne, but not to the seat of government—*there* he finds his mother firmly and pathetically seated; governing in his name, and for him,
with a despotism which he cannot mitigate, and with
a love of power which he cannot cheat. The duchess
is one of those terrible women who, with the softest
manners and the most benevolent intentions, insist on
a despotic carrying out of all their schemes, and who,
representing themselves as on the brink of the grave,
throw the responsibility on their contradictors of the
fatal consequences which may ensue from a contradiction. She wields the sceptre, and whenever her son
attempts to argue with her, whenever he shows the
least sign of resistance, her "failing health and shattered nerves" are invoked; she retires behind them,
as the goddess in Homer takes refuge in a cloud.
The whole play is an exhibition of court life and the
petty struggle for power.

It was represented with a verisimilitude perfectly
charming—not simply in the close adherence to external forms, so that one felt oneself at a German
court; but also in the easy naturalness of demeanor
and unforced truth of mimetic expression, which kept
up our illusion of witnessing real events and real people. This is more particularly true of the actress who
played the Grand Duchess—Frau Frieb-Blumauer—
and the actor who played the Oberhofmeister—Herr
Döring. All the performers were quiet and acceptable, but these two were supremely artistic.

Those who remember Mrs. Glover, and can imagine
her rare and unctuous humor added to the refinement
of Madame Plessy, may form a conception of Frau

Frieb-Blumauer's presentation of the pathetic and dignified despot. A quiet regal manner, a subdued but most significant emphasis, a gentle imperiousness which apparently never dreamed of a possible resistance, a delicate inflexion of voice, and wonderful play of feature and of hands, kept us in a state of constant delight, as touch after touch gave fulness of life to the admirable picture. In a part so easily lending itself to caricature as that of a woman falling back upon her "shattered nerves," Frau Frieb-Blumauer never approached exaggeration by look or tone, and yet gave every detail such unobtrusive relief that not a look or tone passed unobserved. Her elocution was a study. The drooping of her eyelids and the play of hands gave surprising point to very commonplace remarks. Not that she ever made what our actors call "a point." There was nothing to "draw the house down." I do not remember that there was one burst of laughter. But she never was on the stage without usurping every one's attention, and from first to last she kept us fluttering with the thrills of pleasure which follow the recognition of artistic truth. I have since been informed shat she is as great in low comedy as in this, the highest comedy, and that she is mistress of all the dialects. Strange as it may seem that this artist, so remarkable for elegance and delicate *nuance*, should also be great in low comedy, I can believe it, for she seemed artist enough for anything not beyond the sphere of her physical organization. At any rate, there can be no hesitation in affirming that the Berlin stage possesses an actress of high comedy such as nothing on our stage (since Mrs. Glover) can in any way approach. Very remarkable also was the performance of Herr Döring. Thirteen years ago I used to see him play Iago, Shylock, Nathan der Weise, and parts of that class. It was only by reference to the playbill that I could persuade myself that the humorous and very old master of the ceremonies was the same Herr Döring; and, as a testimony to the truth of his acting, it may be added that, although not inexperienced in such matters, I was wholly at a loss to guess how much of the age of his aspect and manner might be reality and how much *mask*. His face was old, his voice was old, his back was old, his legs were old. And as thirteen years may bring enormous changes (say from sixty to seventy-three), in my ignorance of what his age might have been when I saw his Iago and Shylock, it was a puzzle to me to form a notion of the degree in which nature assisted art in this very truthful and very droll representation of an old man. Although actors rightly take advantage of every physical peculiarity, youthful or aged, which the better enables them to represent a character, and the audience only cares for the representation, not for the means employed, there is nevertheless an increased enjoyment when art is known to be creating the very means. We do not admire a man for being old, but we admire him for miming age. All my doubts about Herr Döring were cleared up on the following night, when the shriveled, crumpled, tooth-less, pottering old master of the ceremonies gave place to a dignified, firm-backed, powerful man of fifty.

It would be to convey an exaggerated conception of the German stage to allow this notice of what I saw at Berlin to stand as other than exceptional. I saw nothing like it elsewhere, though at Dresden also there was very creditable *ensemble;* and two friends of mine (one a rare artist) speak of an actor they saw at Coburg as possessing remarkable powers in high comedy. They also confirm my impression that in the passionate drama and in the exuberance of low comedy the Germans are at present defective. Let it be added that if the Germans lack the force of tragic emotion and of ebullient fun, they also avoid as a general rule the cold vehemence of rant, and the coarse vehemence of grimace.

The only tragedy I saw was Hebbel's "Niebelungen," which was produced at Dresden during my stay there. Why this remarkable work has remained untouched for six years after its successful production at Weimar, especially when one reflects on the poverty of the German drama, is a managerial mystery, rendered all the more obscure by the fact that the management could believe in the attractiveness of such tedious works (*pace* Shakspeare!) as the "Two Gentlemen of Verona," "The Comedy of Errors," and the "Midsummer Night's Dream," all three of which were performed in as many weeks. This by the way. I had heard Hebbel's trilogy of "The Nie-belungen" spoken of as the finest work produced since Schiller, and was delighted at the chance of seeing it performed. It is a work which would ill bear transplanting from the German soil, being rather a romantic poem than a tragedy, and implying a certain acquaintance with the old mythological world it reproduces. But readers of German will thank me for calling their attention to it, if they have not already anticipated me.

Only the two first parts of the trilogy were performed during my stay at Dresden. The performance was respectable. The actor who took the part of Siegfried was young, handsome, and spirited— unhappily he was incapable of expressing strong emotion, and rushed into loudness on the slightest provocation. The heroines were both wanting in tragic force; but they and three of the other performers spoke the verse with artistic effect, and the play throughout was carried forward without offence —which is saying much.

Thanks to the existence of court theatres, there is still some strenuous effort to keep up the character of the stage, and stem the rush of vulgar appetites towards vulgar food. In Germany, as elsewhere, costumes and bare backs, spectacle and buffoonery, French ingenuity and French frivolity, dancing and comic songs, allure the crowds who have more eye than soul:

Man kommt zu schaun, man will am liebsten sehen.

And as theatres must be filled, the temptation to fill them with what the multitude prefers, rather than with what the multitude ought to prefer, is very strong. The shop windows of Berlin are unhappily

variegated with the photographs of actresses who
have more bust than talent, more impudence than ac-
complishment ; and the lively licentiousness of Offenbach's musical farces draws crowds to the hundredth
performance, just as in unholy Paris: the *cancan*
(which the French police interdict, or used to interdict, in the balls of students and grisettes) being
nightly encored without a murmur raised.   When
one sees what the performances are which fill the
houses released from court control, and forced to rely
solely on the attractiveness of a pretty woman or the
splendor of a *mise en scène*, one is thankful for the existence of theatres not solely directed by the desire
to make money.   Even in these court theatres there
are unmistakable signs of the decay, elsewhere so
patent, in the increasing reliance on slight French
vaudevilles, and hybrid pieces of spectacle, music and
farce.   But at any rate the lover of the drama is not
without some comfort.   There is still a public which
appreciates classical works.   There are still theatres
where classical works form an important part of the
repertory.   Thus, during the five weeks of my stay
at Dresden we had " Egmont," " Fiesco," " The Two
Gentlemen of Verona," " The Comedy of Errors,"
" The Midsummer Night's Dream," and " The Merchant of Venice," with a comedy of Raupach's, Hebbel's tragedy, " The Niebelungen," and a comedy by
Franz on the subject of the Junius Letters (a very
amusing work, full of political spirit, such as would
have excluded it from *our* stage, and only defective
in the surprisingly loose manner with which Sir Philip
Francis kept his secret, so that every one by turns

discovered it, and the actor could never prevent the stagey start and " confusion" whenever the subject of the Junius authorship was approached). And to these works should be added the operas " Oberon," " Don Juan," " The Huguenots," " Robert the Devil," " Masaniello," " Lohengrin," " Tannhäuser," " Der Fliegende Holländer," the only light operas being " L'Elisir d'Amore " and " Czar und Zimmermann." This, it must be owned, is an array of works presupposing a very different audience from that which supports Offenbach and company ; and a similar array might have been seen on the playbills of every other Hof Theater. There was no memorable excellence exhibited by any one actor to stir the higher emotions ; but there was a level respectability which, in comparison with the acting on our stage, might rank as excellence. The stage is still an intellectual amusement in Germany.

The frequent performance of Wagner's operas at the theatre and at popular concerts was to me not a little surprising in the face of the reckless and contemptuous assertions of French and English critics to the effect that Wagner is only supported by a small and noisy clique. The significant fact that after twenty years of extravagant applause and extravagant abuse, when all novelty must long ago have passed away, the various theatres of Germany and the various concert rooms can still find Wagner's music as attractive (I will not say *more* attractive, although that also might be reasonably urged) as the music of Meyerbeer, ought surely to give the critics pause. I do not myself venture to pronounce

an opinion on the vexed question whether this music
is really destined to be the "music of the future," or
whether it is a pretentious and chaotic effort. This
is a question beyond my competence. I may confess
that the music rarely charms me, and that, as far as
my ear in its present state of musical education de-
termines what is exquisite for it, the Wagner music
wants both form and melody. But then a little reflection suffices to remind one how such *negative* judg-
ments, even from far more competent critics, are
liable to complete reversal. It is not many years
since Beethoven was laughed at, and Rossini sneered
at as a flashy, worthless tickler of the popular ear; indeed, an eminent musician once confessed to me that
he had pronounced "the rage in favor of Rossini a
passing folly," adding, "and now I regard him as one
of the greatest musical creators that ever lived."
How Bellini and Donizetti fared, and how Verdi still
fares at the hands of the critics who are exasperated
at the European success of such music, we all know.
Yet these critics, so scornful of Verdi, are even more
irate with Wagner, who offers something quite different from the hackneyed operatic forms. Surely in
their weariness at the commonplaces of the Italian
opera they might be expected to welcome the novelty
of Wagner? Yet no. The very effect to create a
new form is denounced, and a patient hearing is
denied. It is with music as with all the other arts.
Repeat the old forms, and the critics (justly) denounce the want of originality. Present new forms,
and the critics are put out—deprived of their stand-
ards—and denounce the heresy. It is for the public

to discover the real genius in the artist, and it does so by its genuine response to his work.

And here arises the question, How shall we recognize the real "Vox populi" in such a case? What constitutes a discriminating public? For a new philosophy or a new form of art there can at first be only a small minority; but a group of genuine admirers— souls really moved, and responding because moved— implies the existence of larger groups; and whenever we see a new idea steadily increasing its number of adherents, we may be pretty certain that a public is forming which will one day lose all the characters of a sect. The nature of the idea may always circumscribe this public within comparatively narrow limits; thus the philosophy of Kant, or the music of Beethoven, would always be excluded from a vast mass of minds not in themselves insensible to philosophy or music; but the definition of a public does not depend on numbers, it depends on generations— the constant renewal and propagation of kindred minds.

Let us apply this reasoning to the case of Wagner. Little as I, for one, can—at present and after very superficial acquaintance with his works—respond to the enthusiasm which his music excites in many, there is the noticeable fact staring me in the face that many—and an increasing many—*are* enthusiastic about it; that not only musical fanatics proclaim him to be a great genius, but that the musical audiences of Germany crowd the theatres and testify in concert rooms by their applause their enjoyment of these operas which affect me as horribly noisy, very monotonous, and wanting in charm. Why am I to set up my judgment against theirs? If the music does not flatter my ear, I can keep out of its way, unless— which perhaps would be the more prudent course—I cultivated a little self-suspicion, and withheld all per- emptory judgment, finding, firstly, that other and more educated ears detect form and grace where mine detect none; secondly, that I myself occasion- ally recognize very delightful passages, and may therefore expect that on a longer acquaintance I may learn to admire what is now not admirable.

Standing outside the circle I can nevertheless see and admit that a public for Wagner is steadily form- ing. What will be its magnitude or importance no one can pretend to decide. Whether our children will sneer at us for not having recognized Wagner, or whether they will be following some greater genius, is more than anyone should venture to pronounce. But this much seems clear: Wagner has established his claim to a patient hearing. We ought to do our best to appreciate the art he offers us, and not op- pose every performance of his works which would give us the means of appreciating them.

CHAPTER XIV.

THE DRAMA IN SPAIN. 1867.

IF an old hunter is harnessed to a chaise he will trot along quietly enough, careless of the indignity, submitting like a philosopher to his altered condition in life; but he must not hear the hounds, nor see the scarlet coats—no, that is more than equanimous horse-flesh can bear: it fires the old spirit, and away he dashes, chaise and all, over brook and over fence, through field, through mire, straining, snorting, quivering, in a wild excitement which brings back to him the days of his youth.

It is somewhat thus with the old play-goer. He may be invalided, and relapse meekly enough into the philosopher meditating on the amusements in which he ceases to participate. He becomes quite at his ease respecting "invitations." No array of terms can express how little his anxiety points in the direction of "At homes." Balls leave him insensible to their attractions. Lectures and entertainments placard their allurements in vain. I have known him even resist a sermon. But the sight of a playbill always sends a quiet, pleasurable shock through his nervous system, awakening semi-desires, which only prudence (aided by a well-founded suspicion that the promise of a playbill is a snare) suppresses before they become complete desires. He never quite forgets the foot-lights; never outlives his interest in that scene of dingy splendor, that prosaic fairyland. No amount of bad acting or bad writing altogether disabuses him; he still keeps a little corner of faith in possible en-joyment, and every new name is to him as the herald of a new delight. Hence the irresistible influence of a foreign playbill. All its promises are credible. The leading performers are by a plastic imagination transfigured into representatives of the ideal. The lover has *not* pink eyelids and heterogeneous legs. The interesting heroine is neither mincing nor impu-dent. The light comedian is airy, the low comedian humorous—

> Hope rules a land for ever green!

I had been carefully absenting myself from theatres for some time, having been given to understand that London play-houses were *not* sanatoria; but the sight of a Spanish playbill kindled the smouldering embers into a flame. I had just quitted the sands at St. Se-bastian, after seeing a sunset of indescribable beauty, and turned into the narrow streets of that unimpres-sive town to make a first acquaintance with "las Cosas de España," when a small green placard affixed to one of the walls arrested my eye with "Teatro" in modest caps. Approaching it, I read that an "orig-inal y magnifica comedia en tres actos y en verso," by Don Luis Mariano de Larra (one of the most prolific dramatists of the day), was to be performed that 26th of January. The title was suggestive: "Oros, Copas, Espadas y Bastos"—literally, "Money, Cups, Swords, and Sticks;" or to render it more significantly, "Diamonds, Hearts, Spades, and Clubs."

Not only was I allured by the promise thus held out, as an old play-goer subject to the weakness just described, but also as one who five-and-twenty years ago had made the Spanish drama a particular study, and up to this hour had never had the chance of seeing a Spanish play on the stage. St. Sebastian is not Madrid, neither is it Seville, nor even Barcelona, so that I had no right to expect such a performance as would adequately represent the art. One does not permit a foreigner to see Shakspeare at Ilfracombe, or Sheridan Knowles at Ryde. But being tolerably familiar with the acting of English, French, Germans, and Italians, I thought even the modest troupe of St. Sebastian would afford a glimpse of the national style. Bad acting—as I have had occasion to say—is cruelly common, and singularly uniform on all stages, actors and amateurs being indistinguishable when bad, and seemingly modeled all after the same patterns. Good acting is also uniform; but with that uniformity, which is derived from the fundamental principles of art, there is the great variety of national and personal character. The manners and bearing of a well-bred gentleman are the same in the East as in the West, in the South as in the North of Europe; yet each nation has its distinctive character; and this is seen even through the uniformity of manner.

Some of the universal errors are irritating because

they spring less from inexperience and incompetence than from misguided vanity. Why, for instance, do actors fail to see the absurdity of not looking at the person addressed, as they would look in real life? Why is an impassioned lover, instead of fixing his eyes on the eyes of his mistress, to fix them on the upper boxes, or the side scenes? Such a mistake not only disturbs the illusion of the spectator, but disturbs the artistic imagination of the actor himself by withdrawing it from its direct object. It is because he is thinking of himself and the audience, instead of imaginatively identifying himself with the character he is representing, that his representation is so feeble and confused. If he kept his eyes fixed on the eyes of the person he is addressing, this alone would hinder his thoughts from wandering away from the scene: it would give a poise to his imagination—a poise all the more needful to him because his artistic feeling is feeble; and since spontaneous suggestions fail to sustain his imagination, all external aids become important. It is an invariable characteristic of good actors that they never seem to be conscious of the audience, but always absorbed in the world of which they represent a part; whereas it is the not less invariable characteristic of bad actors that they cannot forget themselves and the audience.

Having disbursed the magnificent sum of six reals (eighteen-pence) for my stall, I did not anticipate anything very remarkable in the art of acting. It was indeed thoroughly mediocre, but inoffensive, and particularly commendable from the absence of that exaggeration which, especially on the English stage, often renders acting intolerable. The *jeune premier* was handsome and gentlemanly ; threw his eyes up at the boxes when he was speaking to his brother or his mistress ; and generally comported himself after the fashion of *jeunes premiers ;* but he neither forced his voice, nor " took the stage." The low comedian was very quiet, and entirely absorbed in his part. The two heroines were indeed without charm, and rolled their eyes as if they hoped to make up in *that* way for any deficiency of talent.

I left the theatre with the impression that, although I had not seen good acting, there was great probability of the Spanish stage furnishing excellent comedians. Taking this St. Sebastian troupe as a starting-point, one could see that the national taste at any rate was healthy, and that whenever an exceptional talent presented itself, it would find a fitting arena. The organization required for fine acting is exceptional, as we see by the rarity of good actors everywhere, in spite of the demand ; but when it does present itself in England it has to contend against a mass of absurd traditions on the stage, and a consequent insensibility on the part of the public. To the " old stager," and perhaps also to the majority of spectators, the quiet demeanor of nature appears like " want of force." I have heard old and favorite actors object to the Affable Hawk of Charles Mathews on the ground of its " wanting weight." The fact is, we have been so long accustomed to heavy beer and brandied wine that pure hops and grape will not stimulate us ; and it is really curious that Southern nations, who habitually gesticulate vivaciously, are less given to gesticulation on the stage than we, who rarely, except on the stage, make use of our hands for expression.

The Englishman seems in general to know no medium between the extreme of apathy and the extreme of exaggeration. His passion runs into rant, his drollery into grotesqueness; he forces his voice, takes the stage, saws the air, and dresses hyperbolically. The low comedian who respects himself and his art, and who seeks effects by quiet drollery rather than by incongruities of costume and outrageous manner, is apt to find the general public tepid in its admiration; and stands but a poor chance against the farcical exaggerations of his rivals.

On the Spanish stage I saw nothing of this coarse buffoonery and ranting violence. Even at St. Sebastian, in the farce, obviously from the French, which followed the comedy, and which the playbill announced as "chistosissima," or "screaming," there was the same absence of turbulent exaggeration. The fun, such as it was, came from words and looks, not from incongruities of costume, or distortions of face and person. It was the same at Barcelona. It was the same at Seville. What has been sneeringly termed the "drawing-room style" everywhere prevails. I do not think it inferior to the "barn style." If the prose of daily life is to be represented on the stage, only such an elevation of the style as is demanded by the laws of stage perspective should be adopted; if the scene be poetical a greater elevation is required; but in either case the fundamental condition is that of representing life; and all *obvious* vio-

lations of the truths of life are errors in art. Prose
on the stage is not to be spoken exactly as in the
street. Verse is not to be spoken as prose. The
natural way of speaking prose or verse is that which,
while preserving the requisite elevation, never allows
us to feel that it is unusual. It is indeed speaking—
not mouthing.

In the comedy, "Oros, Copas, Espadas y Bastos,"
there was a demand made upon the performers which
could not safely be made upon any London troupe,
namely, that of representing a "coat-and-waistcoat
comedy" in verse. The short, tripping verse of the
Spanish drama, interspersed with rhymed passages,
had to be delivered with the ease of prose. There
was, indeed, here and there a little tendency to over-
accentuate the rhythm, but generally it was easily
delivered. Imagine a comedy in blank verse at the
Haymarket!

On the whole, my first experience of Spanish acting
was encouraging, and I looked forward to Seville and
Madrid with great eagerness. Between the comedy
and the farce there was the invariable dance, "bayle
nacional," which the Spaniards seem to consider as
necessary a part of the entertainment as a "comic
song" used to be (happily *used* to be) with us. On
this occasion a tarentella was danced by the very
fattest female in pink that I ever saw dancing: she
flitted about with a certain flopulent energy startling
to behold, and was loudly applauded by her admirers.
Her male companion had the aspect of a wiry, dingy
waiter, very lithe, very agile, and not at all beautiful
to look on.

Don Luis Mariano de Larra is a prolific and popular dramatist, and his comedy, "Oros, Copas, Espadas y Bastos," seemed to be entertaining the audience of every town we entered. I thought it rather dull on a first acquaintance: but as the acting was not remark- able, and as my ears were not sufficiently familiarized with the language to enable me to follow the dialogue closely enough to catch its wit and felicity, I bought the book, and read it before again seeing it performed at Barcelona—where, by the way, it was less well acted than at St. Sebastian. The reader may perhaps like to have some account of this comedy, which delights the audiences of to-day.

The scene opens in the salon of Doña Eduvigis in Madrid. That lady is discussing the subject of mar- riage with her daughters Carmen and Rosa, the former -being a resolute man-hater, the latter a sprightly damsel who has just quitted her convent, regarding men as agreeable animals with whiskers and watch-chains—

> Unos seres con gaban
> y bigotes y reloj—

whose business it is to make love to women, as women's business is to be made love to. Rosa says that when she was in the convent Sister Maria always spoke of man as a venomous animal with large claws, whose sole occupation was the destruction of dam- sels, and that the unfortunate girl who looked at or listened to him was turned into a pillar of salt. "I left the convent," Rosa adds, "saw men, and listened

to them, but was neither torn by their claws, nor
turned into a pillar of salt. So they all please me,
and some please me particularly—

> Por eso me gustan todos . . .
> y alguno me gustan mas."

The old lady sees a bad time of it before her, with
one daughter detesting men too much, and the other
detesting them too little; the more so as a rich uncle
has recently departed from this life (and Ceylon),
leaving his property to the man-hating niece, on condition of her espousing one of her four cousins; and
in the event of her refusal, the money is to go to a
hospital. The four cousins have been invited by
public advertisement to present themselves this very
day.

Old as this idea is, the contrast of the two girls and
the scope for variety of character in the four cousins
are good opportunities for a clever dramatist. But
comedy demands two things in which Spain has always been poor—wit and character. Of the wit in
the present piece all I will say is that it is not spark-
ling. Of the character-drawing you may judge from
the following analysis. By an almost inconceivable
disregard of verisimilitude the author had made the
four cousins, quite needlessly, brothers; yet, not only
are these brothers men of wholly different temperaments and character, but of different *nationalities*—
one is Andalusian, another Arragonese, a third
Castilian. This is thought to be effective contrast!

Don Luis is a cavalry officer, proud of his profession, and especially of—

las magníficas glorias Españolas.

He cites with approval the *mot* of his captain, that you may scent a good soldier at a league's distance—

que al buen soldado hay que olerle
desde una legua.

Whereupon Carmen, who has ironically assured him that his air reveals him to be a dragoon, replies: "It is not, then, singular that I smelt you."

I ought to have stated that after a tedious talk between the three women Carmen is left alone, and Don Luis, entering, asks if he is in the house of Doña Eduvigis, announcing that he presents himself in compliance with the request published in the newspapers, and is anxious to know why he is summoned. This gives him an opportunity of exhibiting his character. But the author's notion of exhibiting character is to make each person describe himself. Don Luis is attracted by Carmen's beauty, but piqued by her epigrams. She quits him to inform her mother of his arrival, and leaves the scene free for the entrance of a second cousin, Casto, who represents the "cups" as Luis represents the "swords" of the title. Casto is a sort of Falstaff of private life, that is, having Falstaff's fat and gulosity, without his wit. The drollery of his part is meant to lie in the fact of his carrying a wine-flask in his pocket, from which in moments of doubt

and timidity he draws inspiration and courage. He
is especially timid in the presence of women.

Having thus presented two of the lovers, the author
now again brings Rosa forward. Luis is struck with
her beauty, but taken aback by her simplicity when,
in answer to some commonplace gallantry, she says,
"How delightful! And shall we be married quickly?"
he gravely checks her and says that her fifteen years
excuse the ingenuousness of the question. "Have I
said anything false?" she asks. "No; but to talk
thus of marrying . . . it is what is never mentioned."
"But if it is *done?*" Don Luis is nonplussed and
refers her to his brother Casto, "a grave personage
who will better explain. . . ." But Casto is relieved
from the embarrassment by the appearance of
Carmen and her mother; and, after the compliments of ceremony are passed, the two other brothers, Blas and José, arrive. Blas is an Arragonese, the
"clubs" of the piece, a rough, plain-spoken, rather
brutal fellow. José is the representative of the
"diamonds," one who believes in the virtue of money.

Doña Eduvigis informs them that they are summoned to her house to hear the will of their uncle,
which she reads aloud—the main point in which I
have already mentioned. Carmen then rises and ad-
dresses them in a frank avowal of her dislike of men
in general. From childhood, when she had to suffer
their horrid beards to brush her face, she has grown
into deeper antipathy to them. If she walks in the
street she never looks behind to see suitors following;
if she goes to a ball she refuses to dance lest a son
of Adam should touch her; if they swear that they

love her she permits them to swear; if they compliment her she is indifferent; and thus her bosom has remained tranquil.

Si voy á la calle	si juran que me aman
no quiero mirar	los dejo jurar ;
por si un barbilindo	si flores me dicen
mi sigue detrás :	á mí me es igual ;
si voy á los bailes,	y de esta manera
renuncio á bailar	mi pecho se está
porque no me togue	sin penas, ni llantos
un hijo de Adan ;	tranquilo y en paz.

To this avowal she adds that if no one of them can win her consent, she is ready to relinquish the inheritance. On her reseating herself, Blas rises and says, "This girl is mad;" and straightway begins to prove that either she does not mean what she says, or that her wits are deficient. But although his tone is insulting, his argument is excessively feeble, and amounts to this, that Carmen will grow old, and regret she has not married. The servant hereupon announces that lunch is ready, and the act feebly ends with this interruption.

In the second act they are again discovered seated, ready to discuss the important question. Blas rises, and in an impertinent speech declares his opinion of the mother and her daughters, in which there is one charming couplet about Rosa, who "feels everything she says, but knows not all she feels"—

Siente todo lo que dice
y no sabe lo que siente.

He then suggests that the four wooers shall honestly paint their own portraits for Carmen's choice. José begins, and with petulant vivacity declares everything vanity except wealth. Casto succeeds, and, patting his huge stomach, declares that therein lies his joy. To rival Heliogabalus in the digesting of huge hams washed down with Malaga is his ambition. The verses, with their involved rhymes, in which this is expressed, are of a buffoonery that delights the pit. But need a remark be made on the incongruity of such burlesque in a coat-and-waistcoat comedy, and especially of the inappropriateness of *such* a presentation of his tastes in one who pretends to the hand of a young heiress?

Luis then rises and avows his military ideal, gratuitously adding that constancy is not his favorite virtue. What Leporello says of Don Giovanni is avowed by Luis of himself.

> La rubia para mí no tiene pero ;
> la morena me robas los sentidos ;
> por la andaluza sin cesar me muero
> y por la de Madrid me dan vahidos.
> Alta me gusta, baja me enamora,
> flaca me da placer, gorda me encanta ;
> me muero por la triste, cuando llora
> me muero por la alegre, cuando canta.

Now comes the turn of Blas, who neither loves nor gambles, neither drinks nor smokes, but has the one defect of irresistible outspokenness.

"I tell everyone both the good and the evil that I see, and as this pleases no one I am always in hot water. Let a painted old woman approach me and

I at once point out the rouge. When I am a man's friend I quarrel with the whole world in his defence; on the contrary, if a man offends me, down comes the stick. I hate ceremony and compliments, never wear gloves, and loathe a dress coat. I rarely pass a day without cracking somebody's skull. People say (but not one in my hearing) that I am a brute; the fact is I am not a stone. If you succeed in pleasing me, Carmen, I will tell you frankly; if not I shall not marry you. But, observe, if we marry, I shall allow no friends or cousins in my house. I tolerate no youth 'who has saved your life,' nor sentimental sigher."

Carmen then replies. If she marries José, he, who thinks only of money, will regard her as a bill of exchange; if Casto, he will turn his eyes from her to a cutlet; if Luis, she will be jealous of every woman; if Blas, she will have to submit to perpetual insults; and she therefore begs to decline them all. Making a reverence she then retires with her mother and Rosa, leaving the four wooers in a speech less astonishment, which is rather singular after their own presentation of their characters. What is to be done? Blas—observe the frank and truthful Blas!—suggests that they should severally write to renounce their pretensions, and all four make furious love to Rosa, the object being to excite Carmen's jealousy. Accordingly each writes a grossly insulting renunciation. Lots are drawn, and Casto has to begin the siege of Rosa's heart. Here occurs a scene of farcical extravagance between the fat and timid Casto, who has to seek courage in the wine flask, and the naïve

Rosa, who is pleased at being made love to even by a
Falstaff. Carmen enters, and Rosa joyfully announces
her conquest. "How," asks the angry Carmen,
"how can you pretend to my hand and make love
to Rosa?" Casto hereupon, with that singular disregard of bienséance which runs through the comedy,
replies, "Because I do not care for you, as this letter
will explain." He gives her the letter and departs.
She reads that her feet are too large, and that one
leg is longer than the other. Luis enters, and at once
begins complimenting Rosa, and handing Carmen his
letter of renunciation. The others follow, and the
act ends with what would make a capital finale for a
comic opera—the four brothers vowing love to Rosa,
each in his characteristic way, and the insulted
Carmen raging like a lioness.

The third act, as is usual in comedies, is feeble.
The two first are not powerful, as the analysis will
have indicated, but at any rate there is movement and
a sort of fun, though more in promise than performance. In the third act the knot is to be untied, and
very clumsily it is untied. The brothers have packed
up their carpet bags and are about to depart, when
Luis discovers that he loves Rosa, and Blas and
Carmen discover, to their surprise, and the surprise of
the spectators, that they also love each other. A
double marriage is arranged, and José and Casto
remain as they were.

It will have been seen that in this comedy there is
neither invention nor dramatic skill. The plot is im-
probable without fantasy, unreal without any imaginative glimpses to compensate for its unreality. The

characters are not even good caricatures. And yet there is a certain dramatic *intention*, which would afford really good actors scope for excellent acting. How they play it in Madrid I cannot say, but at Barcelona it seemed to me as if the actors labored under an intolerable weight, not feeling themselves at all in the characters. At St. Sebastian there was more freedom and more fun.

My first experience of the drama in Spain held out an agreeable prospect of really fine acting when I should have an opportunity of seeing an important troupe; since taking this of St. Sebastian as a standard of confessed mediocrity, it was natural to infer a high standard for Seville and Madrid; but I had only faint hopes of seeing good dramas, unless indeed fortune favored me so far as to bring a work by Zorilla, Gil y Zarate, or Hartzembusch in my way. Alas! French pieces reign in Spain, as in England and Germany; and when "native talent" does enter the arena it is very much like the picador's horse. Spain once furnished Europe with plots and situations as Paris does at present; and early in the present century there seemed a prospect of revival for the Spanish drama. But these hopes have died out. France is still without a rival, and French pieces, more or less adapted, hold possession of all stages. The second piece it was my chance to see, "La Buena Alhaja," was too obviously an importation from the Boulevards, with only the change of Madrid for Paris, and with no omission of the distressing "sentiment" which delights the Boulevards. At Saragossa "Uncle Tom's Cabin" failed to lure me; and at Madrid, during my brief stay there, nothing but French pieces could be seen. At Malaga there was Italian opera. At Granada I could not be tempted to give up the Alhambra by moonlight, more glorious each succeeding night, for the sake of a third endurance of "Oros, Copas, Espadas y Bastos," or for "adaptations." At Cordova the theatre was said to be miserable. Thus Barcelona and Seville were the only cities in which I was enabled to extend my experience, and even there the opportunities were but slight.

On the second day after arriving at Barcelona I was greatly pleased to find among the various theatrical temptations that there was to be a day performance at one of the people's theatres of a mystery-play in the Catalonian dialect—a curious mingling of Spanish and French, and so readily intelligible when written that I concluded it would not be wholly incomprehensible when spoken. The subject was "Los Pastores em Bethelem" ("The Shepherds of Bethlehem "). The theatre was a large tent, and as the day was hot the breeze that swept freely through had a very welcome admission; nor was the smallness of the audience so disagreeable to us as to the manager, especially since every male from eight to nine years upwards incessantly puffed a cigarette; and moreover the flavor of garlic, though stronger, is not sweeter than that of the rose. There was a very fair orchestra, and a not ineffective chorus of angels and demons. The piece itself might have been four centuries old. Probably it was. Except in the matter of scenery and decoration, it was precisely the sort of work which we find in the Chester and Coventry collections; and although I understood extremely little of what the two comic peasants said, I could have no doubt that their fun was precisely the fun of our ancestral clowns.

In Chapter XII. I have spoken of a performance of a mystery at Atwerp, ·by the Ober-Ammergau troupe. This was wholly pantomimic, and wholly serious. But in the "Shepherds of Bethlehem" we had a real drama, with serious and comic acting, chorus, and processions. Satan (though given to straddling) was very energetic. The Archangel Michael was exactly like one of the doll images adorning the churches. But both Satan and the angel were evidently regarded by the audience with earnest awe; and the processions, especially at the wedding of Joseph and Mary ("interspersed with comic business" from the clowns whose wands did not blossom), absorbed them like a religious ceremony. On the whole it was an intensely interesting sight, interesting not only as a relic of the old past, but also as an amusement for the people, which, while it gratified the dramatic instinct, touched their souls to finer issues than could be opened by the vast majority of modern plays. Apart from their religious suggestions, the scenes represented had a pure and poetic significance, which can rarely be found in the theatrical performances of our days. And greatly as our Puritan rigor would be shocked at such representations of sacred history, there can be no doubt that on the simple Catholic populations they have an elevating effect.

Of course it was not on such a stage that one

could expect to see acting. Nevertheless, there was one young actress who played with so much spirit and feeling, and with so little "stage manner," that, had I been a Spanish manager, I should have rescued and educated her, confident of her becoming an artist. There was, also, one young man whose ideal beauty haunts me to this day. I am sorry to say he showed no aptitude for the stage, except that of being quiet and unaffected; but the mere presence of such a lovely head would make the fortune of any play. He was of the Italian rather than the Spanish type; and might have sat to Giorgione for a model. A pale *mat* complexion, exquisitely sensitive nose and mouth, brown curly hair, and soft large eyes, it was just the face we foolishly fancy a poet must have—although experience tells us that poets are really of quite another mould.

Apropos of beauty on the stage, I made a remark on this occasion which was confirmed by subsequent experience, namely, that the great proof of the Spaniards being an unusually handsome people is that even the chorus singers, male and female, are not hideous (as they mostly are all over Europe), but generally good-looking, and often seem to have stepped from the canvas of Velasquez. Recall for a moment the spectacle presented by the chorus in London, Paris, Berlin, Dresden, Milan, Florence! Think of the ungracious women and the mouldy men who range themselves with open mouths and sawing arms, as courtiers, peasants, warriors, and hunters! It has often been a matter of speculation upon what subtle principle of organic development

10

the musical mediocrity, which constitutes the chorus singer, is correlated with countenances so removed from charm, and with figures so ill-adapted to the chisel of Praxiteles.   Musical superiority is frequently found united with great personal beauty; rarely with personal ugliness.   But the musical talent which rises up to, and not above, the level of the chorus seems to lie in a bodily casket which is *not* alluring.   Not so in Spain; or rather let me keep strictly within my experience, and say, not so in Catalonia.   There the men look like noblemen, and the women—

> Avez-vous vu dans Barcelonne
> Une Andalouse au sein bruni,
> Pâle, comme un beau soir d'automne?

I need say no more.

My next experience of the drama (omitting the comic opera, of which more anon) was the most un-fortunate of all.   It was a melodrama, entitled " El Hombre de la Selva Negra;" and this Man of the Black Forest was assuredly the most tedious of all the virtuous proscribed noblemen who have ever paraded their misfortunes on the stage.   From the remorseless length of the unimpassioned dialogue, and the paucity of action, I conclude the piece must have had a German origin; but even German phlegm is fiery compared with the dialogue which a Spanish audience listened to, sublimely patient.   One finds, indeed, that the Spaniard is easily amused.   To sit idly looking on at *anything* seems to him sufficient. Wrapped in his *capa*, or his blanket, with a cigarette under his nose, the mere aspect of the street or prom.

enade is a spectacle; and a procession, show, or theatrical performance of any kind comes like an excitement.

The acting of this dull drama was wholly without marked ability, but it also had the one requisite of moderation. The gentlemen would have disappointed Partridge, for instead of taking the stage like actors they moved and spoke like gentlemen; and the villain would by no means have gained the suffrage of our critics who believe they praise the actor of Iago when they say, "He looked the villain"—that being precisely the thing Iago should not look. It is on this moderation and truthfulness that one may ground a belief in the excellence of Spanish acting. Moderation brings with it the defect of tameness, no doubt; but even this defect is more tolerable in itself than exaggeration, and is less destructive to the art. I must admit the majority of those actors whom I chanced to see were deficient in mimetic power and the sharply defined individuality which characterizes the artist; but not one of them was offensive, and one was of memorable excellence. This one was a performer in a comic opera, or *zarzuela*, poor enough as a singer, but representing a timid and perplexed old nobleman with a richness of humor and significance of look and gesture that recalled Potier and Farren. He was the "one bright particular star" whom it was my luck to see. Not that he held an important position on the stage, but simply because in him the real mimetic faculty which constitutes the actor was allowed its unperverted play. And after seeing him I was strengthened in my expectations of what Seville and Madrid would offer.

Alas! Seville offered me nothing but gentlemanly tameness in a poetic drama, " Un Valle de Lagrimas," of which I have already forgotten everything, and a farce, which may be ascribed as " Box and Cox" with all the fun eviscerated; and Madrid, as I have already stated, offered nothing but poor French pieces, which failed to tempt me.

Whether there are at present any fine actors in Spain I know not, though it is eminently probable. At any rate one feels the steady conviction that the Spanish stage is an excellent arena for the display of genuine art, whenever the artist presents himself. Unhappily the art seems in decadence there, as elsewhere. The national drama has almost ceased to exist. There is no Zorilla, no Hartzembusch now working for the stage. And, apropos of the latter writer, let me direct the attention of any ingenious playwright who can read Spanish to the very effective drama " La Vida por Honra," which would, indeed, require alteration to suit it to our stage, but which presents fine situations and fine "parts" such as a dramatist might make good use of.

The *zarzuela* is the national opera (modeled, indeed, on the French *opéra comique,* and having the same latitude of range), Spanish musicians working with Spanish librettists, and interpreted by Spanish singers. The two specimens I saw were lively and entertaining; one of them, the "Conquista de Madrid," I saw twice, and, in the dearth of agreeable operas, venture to direct the attention of our mana-

gers to it.   Compared with such jingle as Flotow's
" Martha," this "Conquista de Madrid " is a work of
inspiration.   It has a good tenor part, a soprano and
contralto, a fine part for the baritone, and an effective
second tenor.   Animated and piquante the music certainly is ; and if not very original, at any rate it keeps
out of Italian and German ruts.

CHAPTER XV.

I CANNOT pretend to form an estimate of Salvini.
A few years ago I saw him at Genoa in a coat-
and-waistcoat comedy by Scribe (a version of "La
Calomnie"), and was persuaded that he would be well
worth seeing in tragedy. This summer I have .seen
him twice in "Othello," once in the "Gladiator," and
twice in "Hamlet." But this is not enough for a critical estimate; and I will therefore only set down first
impressions.

His performances at Drury Lane have excited an
enthusiasm that recalls the early days of Kean and
Rachel: an enthusiasm which, of course, has been
opposed by some fierce antagonism on the part of
those who are unaffected by his passion, or who dislike his interpretation. It is always so. But for the
most part there has been an acknowledgment of Salvini's great qualities as an actor, even from those who
think his conception of Othello false. My object
here is less to consider his insight into Shakspeare
than his art as an actor. The question of his artistic
skill is one which can be reduced to definite and intelligible principles. The question of insight is one

which fluctuates amid the indefiniteness of personal
taste and experience, complicated by traditional views,
and only in rare cases capable of being fortified by
reference to indisputable indications of the text.
Thus whether Shakspeare paints Othello as a fiery
and sensual African, superficially modified by long
contact with Europeans, or as one with a native chiv-
alry towards woman who is led to marry Desdemona
less from lust than from the gratitude of an elderly
warrior towards a sympathetic maiden who naïvely expresses her admiration, may be left for each person to
settle as he pleases; evidence may be cited in support
of either view, as evidence may be cited to prove
that Othello was "not easily jealous," or that he was
very groundlessly jealous. I remarked on a previous
page the great uncertainty in which Hamlet's madness is left; but whether Shakspeare meant him to be
mad, or feigning madness, nothing can be less equivo-
cal than the indications of a state of cerebral excitement in speech and conduct, and this the actor ought
to represent.

These two examples point out the different attitudes which criticism must take with regard to the
actor's interpretation. In the first case the critic is
impertinent if he thrusts forward *his* reading of the
text as that which the actor is bound to follow; the
more so when a little reflection should suggest a
modest hesitation as to whether on the whole the
actor who has given long and continuous study to the
part in all its details, and with mind alert to seize
every hint and settle every intonation, is not more
likely to be right than one who has had no such

pressing motive, and whose conception of the part has been formed fitfully from occasional readings, or occasional visits to the theatre. In the second case, the critic has the plain indications of the text which he can say the actor has disregarded; that is a question which can be argued on definite and intelligible principles. No actor is to be blamed for not presenting *your* conception of Hamlet, Othello, or Macbeth; but he is justly blamed when he departs from the text such as all men understand it. You may not think that Othello was a man of fierce animal passion, but you know that Othello stabbed himself and did *not* cut his throat.

It is not therefore Salvini's reading of Othello that I shall touch upon, so much as the skill with which his reading is personated. I went to the first performance prepared by long familiarity with the play, and biased by very vivid recollections of Edmund Kean; and came away with the feeling that, although in certain passages manifestly inferior to Kean, the representation as a whole was of more sustained excellence.

His noble bearing, and the subtle music of his varied declamation in the scene before the senate, and the play of expression while Brabantio accuses him—when Desdemona appears—and when she replies to the Doge, were confirmations of my high expectation. Here it was evident that the primary requisites of the art were in his power. He had vocal and facial expression. It is only those accustomed to critical analysis who have the least idea of the rarity of these two qualities, especially the former.

While everyone understands that it is a primary requisite in a singer that he should not only have a voice, but know how to *sing*, very few seem to suspect that it is not less a primary requisite in an actor that he should know how to *speak*. The consequence is that very few actors do know how to speak, and scarcely any of them can speak verse.

In the scene at Cyprus, whatever objections might be urged against the *kind* of passion he expresses, there could be no doubt respecting the truth with which it was expressed. I did not think his dismissal of Cassio good. The memory of Kean here obtruded itself. But the temptation scene, from first to last, was a magnificent display of the resources of his art. The subtle and varied expression of uneasiness growing into haggard grief—desiring to learn all that was in Iago's mind, yet dreading to know it—trying to conceal from him the effect of his hints, and more and more losing all control—could not have been more artistically truthful. It was profoundly tragic, because profoundly natural. He gave a novel and felicitous interpretation to the passage, " Excellent wretch! perdition catch my soul but I do love thee, and when I love thee not "—here a momentary pause was followed by a gesture which *explained* the words —" chaos is come again "—the world vanishing into chaos at such a monstrous state of feeling. The " Farewell the tranquil mind " was not comparable to the deep, manly, and *impersonal* pathos of Kean (I will explain the epithet presently), and it seemed to me *over*-acted; the same remark applies to the " Had it pleased heaven to rain affliction on me." I missed, also, the fiery intensity of Kean's " Blood, Iago, blood," and " I'll tear her to pieces," and his searching tenderness in " Oh the pity of it, Iago." But the whole house was swept along by the intense and finely graduated culmination of passion in the outburst, "Villain, be sure you prove," etc., when, seizing Iago and shaking him as a lion might shake a wolf, he finishes by flinging him on the ground, raises his foot to trample on the wretch—and then a sudden revulsion of feeling checks the brutality of the act, the *gentleman* masters the *animal,* and with mingled remorse and disgust he stretches forth a hand to raise him up. I remember nothing so musically perfect in its *tempo* and intonation, so emotionally perfect in expression, as his delivery of this passage—the fury visibly growing with every word, his whole being vibrating, his face aflame, the voice becoming more and more terrible, and yet so completely under musical control that it never approached a scream. Kean was tremendous in this passage; but Salvini surpassed him.

In the fourth act he was also fine, but I missed the evidence of what (at page 18) I called the ground-swell of subsiding passion. After the dread conviction of Desdemona's guilt has once entered his soul, Othello can never for a moment pass from out of the shadow of that calamity. He may force himself to appear calm—but the calmness should be shown to cover a deep wrath and woe. I did not feel this in Salvini's calmness. But how fine his sarcasm, and his shrinking from Desdemona's approach! with what a shudder of disgust he quits Emilia!

In the fifth act my admiration ceased. Except the passionate cry when he learns Desdemona's innocence, and the dreadful way in which he paces to and fro, like a lion in his den, before he murders her, I remember little in this act which satisfied me. The frequent objections that have been urged respecting the melodramatic introduction of thunder and lightning, and his using a short scimiter to cut his throat, instead of a dagger to stab himself, weigh but little. The lightning had better have been omitted; and the attempt at "local color" with the scimiter was a two-fold mistake—in the first place it is in contradiction with the text, in the second place not half a dozen of the audience could be expected to know that stabbing was not an Oriental mode of suicide. But even admitting all that has been said against the "gross realism" of the dying struggles, it would only constitute one defect in an act which seemed to me to sin in far deeper respects. My objection to Salvini's fifth act is that it is underfelt and overacted; or let me say it seemed to me mistakenly conceived, and did not impress me as having the guidance of consistent emotion; it therefore erred as all acting must err under such circumstances, trying to replace a massive effect by a multiplicity of varied effects. We observe this also in writers who, having no inward impulse of emotion, or no conviction, seek effects from the outside: they endeavor to dazzle or persuade by artifices, and

Hide by ornament the want of art.

Salvini's Othello, in this act, was not a man who has resolved on killing his wife as a solemn sacrifice.

There was nothing of the dread calm of a supreme resolve. He alternately raged and blubbered—and was never pathetic.

And here I may recur to what was touched on just now, the deficiency of pathos in his acting. His pathetic tones are not searching: there are no tears in his voice; instead of that he is unpleasantly tearful—which is a totally different thing. Tragic pathos to be grand should be *impersonal.* Instead of our being made to feel that the sufferer is giving himself up to self-pity, we should be made to see in his anguish the expression of a general sorrow. The tragic passion identifies its suffering with the suffering of mankind. The hero is presented less as moaning over his lot, exclaiming: " I am so miserable!" than as moaning over his and the common lot, exclaiming: "O, this misery!" Even in daily life you may observe that sympathy with grief is apt to be somewhat checked when the sufferer is greatly preoccupied with the calamity as *his;* the more he pities himself the less you pity him. Grief, however intense, however wild in its expression, when borne with a sense of its being part of our general heritage, excites the deepest sympathy; we feel most keenly *for* the sufferer in feeling *with* him.

I cannot say that I much enjoyed " The Gladiator." There were one or two fine moments, and the performance was interesting as showing Salvini in a very different light, showing how artistically he endeavored to *personate*—that is, to speak through the character. Nothing could be more unlike his Othello. But it seemed to me that all the defects noticeable in the

Othello were exaggerated in the Gladiator; and the overacting and self-pity left me cold. The main cause of this was doubtless the absence of any genuine dramatic material to work upon. The play is contemptible—a succession of conventional "motives," such as seduce feeble writers who vainly imagine they can be effective by heaping situation on situation, robing their characters in all the frippery of the stage. One may say of the play, and of Salvini's acting, what Johnson said of a poem when Boswell asked him if it had not imagination: "No, sir; there is in it what *was* imagination once." Salvini showed us what had been dramatic expression: and so powerful is his mastery that many spectators accepted the conventional signs; just as many readers accept for poetry the splendid images and poetic thoughts which inferior writers gather from other writers far and wide, instead of expressing poetical feelings of their own.

I do not blame Salvini for not having interested me in the Gladiator, for I do not think that any actor could have succeeded with such a patchwork. But I must blame his overacting—the apparent determination to get a multiplicity of effects out of materials which might have been more simply and massively presented. An illustration may be cited from his first scene. In telling the hideous history of his child, ripped from its mother's womb, he turned the narrative into a dramatized presentation, going so far as to repeat the words of the sorceress in high womanly tones. In his gestures there is always an excess in this direction: an excess which would not be felt indeed by Italians, since they are much given to what may be called pictorial gesture; but I cannot think it consistent with fine art, being, as it is, a remnant of the early stages of evolution, wherein gesture is descriptive, and not, as in the higher stages, symbolical: it bears the same relation to the expressive gestures of cultivated minds that picture-writing bears to the alphabet.

With this qualification, and considering him as an Italian, Salvini's gestures are fine, though, to my thinking, redundant. His tones and looks — the actor's finest gestures—are singularly varied and effective.

My disappointment at his performance of the Gladiator abated my expectations of his Hamlet, for which part his physique so obviously ill-fitted him. Yet here—because he had again genuine dramatic material to work upon—the actor's art was once more superbly shown. It was not Shakspeare's Hamlet, one must admit; the many-sidedness of that strange character was sadly truncated—the wit, the princely gaiety which momentarily plays over the abiding gloom, the vacillating infirmity of purpose, the intellectual over-activity, were "conspicuous by their absence." The play had been cut down to suit Italian tastes. Nevertheless, I think of all the Hamlets I have seen Salvini's is the least disappointing. Of all that I have seen, it has the greatest excellences. The scenes with the Ghost erred, I think, psychologically in depicting physical terror rather than metaphysical awe; but this is the universal defect; and Salvini's terror was finely expressed. The soliloquies were quiet, and were real soliloquizings, except that every now and then too much was *italicized* and *painted out:* so that he seemed less one communing with himself than one illustrating his meaning to a listener. The scene with Polonius, " Words, words," was so admirable that it deepened regret at the mutilation of the text which reduced this aspect of Hamlet to a transient indication. The scene with Ophelia was a revelation. Instead of roaring and scolding at her like other actors, with a fierce rudeness which is all the more incomprehensible that they do not represent Hamlet as mad, Salvini is strange, enigmatical, but always tender; and his "To a nunnery go " is the mournful advice of a broked-hearted lover, not the insult of a bully or angry pedagogue. This tenderness, dashed with insurgent reproaches, runs through the interview with his mother; and the most pathetic tones I have heard him utter were in the broken huskiness of his entreaties to her to repent. The growing intensity of emotion during the play-scene culminates in a great outburst of triumphant rage as he wildly flings into the air the leaves of the manuscript he has been biting a second before, and falls exhausted on Horatio's neck. No one who witnessed that truthful expression of powerful emotion could help regretting the excision of so many passages of "wild and whirling words" in which Hamlet gives vent to his cerebral excitement.

Powerful and truthful also was his acting in the scene where he catches the King at prayer. But dull beyond all precedent was the talk at Ophelia's grave! The close was magnificent. No more pathetic death has been seen on the stage. Among its many fine touches there was the subtle invention of making the dying Hamlet draw down the head of Horatio to kiss him before sinking into silence: which reminds one of the "Kiss me, Hardy," of the dying Nelson. And this affecting motive was represented by an action as novel as it was truthful—namely, the uncertain hand blindly searching for the dear head, and then faintly closing on it with a sort of final adieu.

There are two points which struck me as lessening the effect of this otherwise rare performance: the first was a tearful tendency, sometimes amounting almost to a whining feebleness; the second, nearly connected with this, was a want of perfect consistency in the presentation. There was a dissonance between the high plaintive tones and the massive animal force, both of person and voice—it was an operatic tenor, or *un beau ténébreux*, grafted on the tragic hero: an incongruous union of the pretty with the grand.

But I am only noting first impressions, and I will not by insisting on faults seem ungrateful to the great artist, who has once more proved to us what the art is capable of. Make what deductions you please— and no artist is without his comparative deficiencies —you must still admire the rare qualities of the tragedian. He has a handsome and eminently expressive face, graceful and noble bearing, singular power of expressing tragic passion, a voice of rare beauty, and an elocution such as one only hears once or twice in a lifetime: in the three great elements of musical expression, tone, timbre, and rhythm, Salvini is the greatest speaker I have heard.

THE END.

INDEX.